In 1937, after the destruction of his apartment in Casa de las Flores by Franco's soldiers, dejected Pablo Neruda returned to Chile. He needed a remote place in which to reflect on what had happened and to write an epic 'Canto General de Chile', which would also be the manifestation of his attempt to produce *impure poetry.* One year later he bought a small stone construction on the Pacific Ocean, which he would continuously expand and modify until the day of his death, eleven days after the coup d'etat of Augusto Pinochet which again destroyed his home.

House in Isla Negra, Chile, c. 1956.
Photo: Manuel Solimano. Pablo Neruda's Foundation Archive

It was around 1941 when Ralph Erskine erected a small cabin in forested land near Stockholm. It was a minimal domestic structure, later known as 'the Box'; his first attempt as an architect to immerse in the material reality. Upon the completion of the cabin in 1942, the Erskine family moved there to escape German bombings that were terrorizing London. Erskine's first architectural project was thereby little more than a place in which to survive, yet, also an experience which facilitated the reflection on a new future through daily interaction with nature.

Ralph Erskine, The Box, Lissma, Sweden, c. 1941–1942.
(Picture of the 1989–1993 reconstruction near Drottningholm, Sweden).
Photo: Francisco González de Canales

In 1941 Charles and Ray Eames moved to Los Angeles, hoping for a United States military victory, which would allow them to conceive a sunny post-war life in the place that was especially privileged by the development of war technologies. The Eameses constructed a domestic unit in the Pacific Palisades, isolated between the Pacific Ocean and an eucalyptus grove. For years its interior spaces were being intensively manipulated by means of reflections, Polaroid cameras and Mexican artisanship.

Charles and Ray Eames, Case Study #8, Pacific Palisades, Santa Monica, California, 1945–1949. **Photo: Francisco González de Canales**

In 1942, following the German invasion, Max Ernst fled Paris to spend years in and around Arizona, New Mexico and California, seduced by mysterious beauty of the countryside. Few years later he settled in a modest cottage in Sedona, Arizona, which he built with his own hands, placing a stone over a stone for more than six years. From then on, his art changed radically: his surrealist landscapes started to meld with the actual desert in which he lived.

Max Ernst. House in Sedona, Arizona, c. 1946

One year later, in 1943, when the Germans occupied the north and centre of Italy, Curzio Malaparte moved to a prominent cliff in Capri, where Adalberto Libera had designed for him a house on top of the rocky precipice. Once situated, Malaparte modified the project to suit his own form of life, working directly with local masons on each detail and on an overall expression of his lifestyle. The result reduced the distance between his life and his house to the minimum. Malaparte irrefutably constructed what would be *una casa comme me* (a house like me).

Malaparte House, Punto Masullo, Capri, c. 1943.
Photo: Benjamin Goñi

Once the war had ended, in 1946, Lina Bo and Pietro María Bardi emigrated from Italy to Brazil in hopes of escaping the devastation and trauma caused by the Second World War in their home country. For five years, until 1951, they constructed a hybrid house made of glass, brick and metal on the outskirts of São Paulo. It was a sort of a cabinet-house or a backpack-house, in which it was possible to store away everything they owned. Just as Lina Bo had drawn, the house's final ability was to disappear, to get lost in the wild, engulfed by vegetation, as an unavoidable consequence of the exposure to the fierce, anthropophagic wilderness of Brazil.

Lina Bo Bardi's Glass House in Morumbi, São Paulo, 1949–1951.
Photo: Francisco González de Canales

It was around 1949 when Juan O'Gorman, disappointed by the post-revolutionary politics and the development of Mexico City after the Second World War, moved from his functionalist house constructed at the beginning of the 1930s – and located close to the one he had built for his friend Diego Rivera – to a cave of volcanic origin in the foothills of El Pedregal. He lived there until 1967, and while his wife organized and attended the surrounding flora, O'Gorman adorned the solidified magma with his colourful stones.

Juan O'Gorman's house in El Pedregal, Mexico City, 1949–1967.
Photographic Archive Manuel Tuissant, Instituto de Investigaciones Estéticas, UNAM, Mexico

In 1956, disenchanted with the urban growth of large Australian cities and the devastation of the aboriginal populations, Wilfred and Ruth Lucas decided to move to the outskirts of Castlecrag, New South Wales, to build for themselves a house in the dense forest surrounding them. They constructed a kind of a tree house, like those made for children in gardens, but designed with the aim of investigating new lightweight and reversible solutions in nature. Each element and piece of furniture was developed through intense research, in the process of a continual negotiation between bodies, objects, nature and forms of life.

Ruth and Willfred Lucas in their "tree-house" in Castlecrag, Australia, c. 1956.
Photo: David Moore

Only one year later, at the height of the Cold War, around 1957, Alison and Peter Smithson started a series of trips across the rural England, rejecting the United Kingdom's adoption of radical consumerist politics and the deceptive development of the country's new towns. In 1959 they started the construction of a small cottage of wood and glass, erected on an old, rural stone partition. Their experience there, which lasted more than twenty years, would be the basis for the Smithsons' redefinition of the art of inhabitation.

Alison and Peter Smithson building their Upper Lawn Pavilion in Fonthill, Wiltshire, UK, c. 1961. **Photo: Smithson Family Collection, London**

Look in any traditional reference book on the history of modern architecture and you will find many pages dedicated to the historical avant-gardes and the formation of the Modern Movement till the mid-1930s, and many more dedicated to its reconstruction and expansion after World War II. It seems that in the 1940s nothing important occurred. However, the period between the end of the 1930s and the end of the 1950s was especially fruitful for a new kind of freer and more uninhibited experiments. During this time marked by war and exile, rationing and dissatisfaction, architects and artists deployed radical individual experiments through modestly scaled projects in order to commit to new critical agendas and conditions for future inhabitation. Although highly diverse in their aims and scope, their trials can be grouped together as responses distinguished for their extremely testing means, in which the experimenter is experimenting with him-/herself.

Experiments with Life Itself

Radical Domestic Architectures between 1937 and 1959

Francisco González de Canales

Index

Prologue

This text was published for the first time in the magazine *RA* 10, University of Navarra, 2008.
I would like to thank for the support of the Junta de Andalucía, the La Caixa Foundation, the University of Sevilla and the Harvard Graduate School of Design, that made this research possible. I would also like to thank for the comments and help of my colleagues: Nuria Álvarez Lombardero, Sibel Bozdogan, Adrian Gorelik, K. Michael Hays, Juan José Lahuerta, Rafael Moneo, José Ramón Moreno Pérez, Andrés Perea, Víctor Pérez Escolano, Juan Luis Rodríguez, Ricardo Sánchez Lampreave, Hashim Sarkis, Graciela Silvestri, Eduardo Subirats, Jorge Tárrago,and many more that I have forgotten but hope they forgive me.

Pablo Neruda and Delia del Carril in Isla Negra, Ralph Erskine in Lissma, Charles and Ray Eames in the Pacific Palisades, Max Ernst and Dorothea Tanning in Sedona, Curzio Malaparte in Punto Masullo, Lina Bo and Pietro María Bardi in Morumbi, Juan and Helen O'Gorman in El Pedregal, Ruth and Wilfred Lucas in Castlecrag, Alison and Peter Smithson in Fonthill... Although truly heterogeneous in their origins and outcomes, this selection of diverse cases completed between the end of the 1930s and the end of the 1950s exemplifies the configuration of a phenomenon which I call domestic self-experimentation, defined as the individual and multiple production of fragmented and highly experimental practices on the peripheries of the existing social order.[1] These forms of domestic self-experimentation can be characterized by a set of common traits and peculiarities.

First of all, they are radically experimental because those who practice and carry them out are also the objects of their experiments. They are experimenting on themselves, aware of the fact that they are the only reliable witnesses of their investigative work. Such a definition echoes the notion of experimenting with oneself that has been developed lately by Peter Sloterdijk, in which the author converts him-/herself simultaneously into a scientist and his/her guinea pig.[2] In the same way that Samuel Hahnemann – the father of homeopathic medicine – thought that the doctor was obliged to poison himself with anything he would prescribe to his patients,[3] for Sloterdijk, 'the author that is useful to us is the one that contaminates himself with the materials with which he works'.[4] According to Sloterdijk, not only are we 'condemned' to depart from the paradigm of modern scientific experimentation but we have to make of the experimentation a personal, individual and dispersed process. Each one of us has to become 'a subject involved in the adventure of his own self-preservation, a subject that wants to

1 — This definition does not exclusively refer to the cases described above; nonetheless, these cases justify its existence.
2 — Peter Sloterdijk, *Selbstversuch. Ein Gespräch mit Carlos Oliveira* (Munich und Viena: Carl Hanser, 1996), 145–6.
3 — Sloterdijk compares this procedure with that of Samuel Hahnemann, considered to be the founder of homeopathic medicine. In 1792, Hahnemann started experimenting with substances that he first administered to himself and later to his family, students and volunteers. Hahnemann discovered that the reactions and bodily responses to these substances were different in each individual. The combination of reactions to each substance Hahnemann tested formed a kind of panel that he used to determine the multiple medical properties of the substance. Hahnenmann main ideas are gathered in his *Organon of Medicine*. Samuel Hahnemann, *Organon of Medicine* (Blaine, WA: Cooper Publishing, 1996).
4 — Peter Sloterdijk, *Selbstversuch. Ein Gespräch mit Carlos Oliveira*, 146.

determine on experimental grounds what kind of life is the best for him/her', configuring for him-/herself the complete horizon of existence.[5] Despite the unavoidable individualism of the domestic self-experimentation, we should interpret it as much more than just a mere personal reaction. Rather, it is a confluence of practices which, while undoubtedly heterogeneous and distinct, come together to configure a constellation of symptoms or reactive actions that, in turn, define the framework of particular problems and a new sense of collective experimentation.[6] This convergence, or an *array of experimentation,* can be better understood using the concept that Bruno Latour has called *collective experimentation,* in which, from multiple, varied experiments, 'the collective has to explore the questions of the number of entities to be taken into account and integrated, through a grouping process whose protocol is defined by the power to follow up'. In our case it is the array of diverse self-experimentations that needs to be considered in order to reorganize the common.[7]

Secondly, this experimentation is a practice which has no end. It manifests itself as a *modus vivendi* which should be deployed

5 — Peter Sloterdijk, *Selbstversuch. Ein Gespräch mit Carlos Oliveira,* 34; see, in general, 32–6.

6 — Bruno Latour, *Politics of Nature,* Catherine Porter (trans.), (Cambridge: Harvard University Press, 2004), 238. See also: ' *Power to follow up*: it seeks the test path that allows collective experimentation to explore the question of common worlds; it is procedural and not substantive; so long as it does not presuppose mastery, it is thus synonymous with the art of governing.' Latour, 242.**

7 — There is an affinity between these ideas and the post-operaist notion of *multitudo* (multitude) which – in the particular theorization of philosopher Toni Negri – takes the subversive power of the Marxist notion of *general intellect* in order to explain the potential of such disperse reactive practices. Within the notion of multitude, it is the multiple but individual production of subjectivity that constitutes the common. 'The people is one. The population, of course is composed of numerous different individuals and classes, but the people synthesizes or reduces these social differences into one identity. The multitude, by contrast, is not unified but remains plural and multiple. ... The multitude is composed of a set of singularities—and by singularity here we mean a social subject whose difference cannot be reduced to sameness, a difference that remains different. The component parts of the people are indifferent in their unity; they become an identity by negating or setting aside their differences. The plural singularities of the multitude thus stands in contrast to the undifferentiated unity of the people.' Antonio Negri and Michael Hardt, *Multitude: War and Democracy in the Age of Empire* (New York: Penguin, 2004), 99.

continuously. This aspect is not understood only as a circumstantial fact but also – more accurately – as a chronic state. It is impossible to date these architectural endeavours as the traditional written history has been accustomed to, since it is not possible to assign to them a specific date or even an interval of dates that would mark the beginning and the execution of each project. The experiments we are speaking of continuously expand and adapt, and in none of the cases would it be possible to say that the execution of the work concluded in a particular moment. Nor would it be realistic to decide in which moment the project arose, because these experimentations – both self-intoxicating and detoxifying – live in parallel to their constructors/users. They represent a constant flux of modifications, amplifications and reductions that do not occur in a linear fashion. If these structures had ever been considered completed, they would have been demoted, abandoned or demolished.

Thirdly, these experimentations extend to the peripheries of the civic urban order. That is to say, they are located outside of normal civic regulations and were generated as a responsive practice. The particular circumstances from which these domestic self-experimentations arise are inseparably tied to the times when the illusion of progress seems to have vanished in the extermination camps. Genocide and occupation provoke a historic regression which, as Giorgio Agamben has indicated, brings back the sordid figure of the 'homo sacer'.[8] To a high degree, the emergence of these particular cases of the abandonment of civic life and the openness to domestic experimentation in nature directly relates to a very particular historical period. It would be fair to say that the domestic self-experimentation was the convergence of individual reactions to the surge of European totalitarianisms, World War II and the Cold War. Nevertheless, during these distinct periods, relationship between the conflict

8 — 'Homo sacer is unsacrificeable, yet he may nevertheless be killed by anyone. The dimension of bare life that constitutes the immediate referent of sovereign violence is more original than the opposition of the sacrificeable and the unsacrificeable, and gestures toward an idea of sacredness that is no longer absolutely definable through the conceptual pair (which is perfectly clear in societies familiar with sacrifice) of fitness for sacrifice and immolation according to ritual forms. In modernity, the principle of the sacredness of life is thus completely emancipated from sacrificial ideology, and in our culture the meaning of the term "sacred" continues the semantic history of homo sacer and not that of sacrifice (and this is why the demystifications of sacrificial ideology so common today remain insufficient, even though they are correct). What confronts us today is a life that as such is exposed to a violence without precedent precisely in the most profane and banal ways.' Giorgio Agamben, *Homo Sacer: Sovereign Power and Bare Life,* Daniel Heller-Roazen (trans.), (Stanford: Stanford University Press, 1998), 75.

and domestic self-experimentation has not remained constant. In the beginning domestic self-experimentation was a reaction to direct effects of warfare; for example, as the search for a refuge from bombings and the military occupation. In the later stages, to the contrary, the relationship arises from the other, less apparent aftermath, such as the escape from the disenchantment with the promises of post-war development or from the strained climate of the Cold War.

c. 1937

It is my intention to define a certain understanding of the concept of domestic self-experimentation beginning with 1937. There is a reason for choosing this date. Architecturally, it refers to the breakup of the pre-war CIAM (Congrès Internationaux d'Architecture Moderne) during the Paris World Exposition. Not only did this event demonstrate an insurmountable crisis of architectural culture[9] but, above all, a profound general socio-cultural and political crisis that would acquire an international character catalyzed by the deepening of the socialist/fascist conflict in the Spanish Civil War and the increasing tension between totalitarian superpowers of the USSR and the Third Reich.[10] In order to situate this crisis, I would like to use Giorgio Agamben's words:

It was in some ways already evident starting with the end of the First World War that the European nation-states were no longer capable of taking on historical tasks and that peoples themselves were bound to disappear. We completely misunderstand the nature of the great totalitarian experiments of the twentieth century if we see them only as carrying out of the nineteenth century nation-states' last great tasks: nationalism and imperialism. The stakes are now different and much higher, for it is a question of taking on as a task the very factual existence of

9 — Parallel to the organization of CIAM V in Paris (*Logis et Loisirs* / Dwellings and Leisure), Le Corbusier and Pierre Jeanneret worked on their highly ambitious Pavilion des Temps Nouveaux for the 1937 World Exposition. More than 100 architects, artists and intellectuals collaborated on the design that Le Corbusier started conceiving in 1931 and that was intended to host CIAM and other debates on urbanism. The Pavilion des Temps Nouveaux epitomized the last attempt of an integrative modernist practice as an extension of the avant-gardes before World War II. See Danilo Udovicki-Selb, 'Le Corbusier and the Paris Exhibition of 1937: The Temps Nouveaux Pavilion', *Journal of the Society of Architectural Historians,* 56.1 (Mar. 1997), 42–63.

10 — The face-to-face confrontation of the German and Soviet pavilions during the 1937 Paris Exposition has been often alluded to as an aesthetic demonstration of the socialist/fascist conflict, relevant not only in the political but also the cultural terms of the time.

peoples, that is, in the last analysis, their bare life. Man has now reached his historical telos and, for a humanity that has become animal again, there is nothing left but the de-politicizing of human societies by means of the unconditioned unfolding of the *oikonomia*, or the taking on of biological life itself as the supreme political (or rather apolitical) task.[11]

11 — Giorgio Agamben, *The Open: Man and Animal*, Kevin Attell (trans.), (Stanford: Stanford University, 2004), 76.

In other words, when the nation-states are at the point of near collapse, the only remarkable task left to be accomplished is the total management of political and biological life, and this is precisely what the European totalitarianisms tried to do. Within this historical frame, domestic self-experimentation should be understood as an answer to the total (biological and political, or: biopolitical) management; as an alternative set of practices that seek new forms in order to reorganize multiple cultures and natures. According to Agamben, there is also a transfer from the totalitarian movements to the victors of World War II (principally the United States) that did not manifest itself only as the inheritance of the supreme task of the total management of the social masses but also as a specific inheritance of the War Culture.[12] This includes skills in the use of telecommunications systems and other means of communication developed during the war, which would enormously affect the living conditions in the Cold War society. Control of the telecommunications and the use of radio as a means of complete propaganda – the construction of a second parallel nature for the total management of the masses (as Goebbels had conceived it) – would open the path in the post-war period to the development of television as the key means of reproduction of socio-political programs.[13]

12 — Giorgio Agamben, *Homo Sacer*, 151–229. It is relevant to note here that this war culture does not only mean a revolution in heavy industries – in the means of production and reconstruction of a world in ruins – but it is also characterized by an extraordinary developments in the social sciences. In 1941 Adorno and Horkheimer are finishing their revolutionary work of critical theory *Dialectics of Enlightenment* while Levi-Strauss is collecting in the NY Public Library the data for his *Structure of Kinship*, the foundational text of structural anthropology.

13 — McLuhan says on Goebbels: 'Radio provided the first massive experience of electronic implosion, that reversal of the entire direction and meaning of literate Western civilization'. Marshall McLuhan, *Understanding Media: The Extensions of Man* (New York: New American Library, 1964), 300.

Continuing with the Agamben's thought, also a revision of the idea of the end of history can help establish a conceptual framework for this period. Even though the concept has been used profusely by anxious theorists of our 'post' era, Francis Fukuyama, for example,[14] it also brings us back to the first French existentialists, in particular to the figure of Alexandre Kojève, who popularized the term, along with Sartre, Merleau-Ponty and Bataille. Kojève reread Hegel from an anthropological point of view, in which the end of history meant the end of obstacles that up until then had been interposed between the man and his control of his own destiny.[15] At the end of history the situation would crystallize as follows: after God has been 'removed from power' and nature has been completely tamed, there no longer exist any impediments to the totalitarian human order.[16]

14 — I am referring to his polemical work *The End of History and the Last Man* (New York, Toronto: Free Press and Maxwell Macmillan, 1992).

15 — To situate this particular event in French philosophy, it is relevant to revisit: Vincent Descombes, *Le Même et l'autre: quarante-cinq ans de philosophie française (1933–1978)* (Paris: Minuit, 1979), 27–72.

16 — There are also interesting reflections on the notion of the 'end of history' in Peter Sloterdijk's texts. See Peter Sloterdijk and Hans-Jürgen Heinrichs, *Neither Sun Nor Death*, Steve Corcoran (trans.), (Cambridge, MA and London: Semiotext(e), 2011), 123–135.

The man at the end of history has been twice expropriated of what modernity used to objectify as his exterior. Neither can the old nature act as an external environment defining an object (because everything has already been included in the artificial environment), nor is history capable of recreating it since history itself has been annulled as an artificial transfer between the past and the future, frozen in the world without a horizon or an idea of progress. As Sartre would say, all that remains for the human being is his/her own existence – that is, actions of his/her own making, about which the only assertions that one can make is that an acting individual exists or that the action is taking place. The only possible testimony is the event itself and any further speculation is a pure transcendental illusion.[17] As a result, any proposed alternative to this order must stem from the individual, marginal and private experimentation. Hence, the architects committed to such alternative would have to start by experimenting with themselves as the only reliable witnesses.[18] They would be forced to experiment with their own lives and with their relational bounds with the spaces and environments they built in solitude.

In the climate of scattered individualism some architects and artists begin to escape to nature;

17 — '*Mardi*: Rien. Existé'. (*Tuesday*: Nothing. Existed). This laconic entry to Antoine Roquentin's diary defines this particular state of mind. Jean-Paul Sartre, *La nausée* (París: Gallimard, 1938), 144.

18 — Subsequent to the collapse of the 'perfect moments', or 'privileged situations', as referred to in *La nausée* (162–9), appear different existentialist responses to ratify this principle of action. From the *beat-snickers* to the Situationists, the *situation*, the happening, the event, is the only thing that can be ascertained: either there is an event, or there is not.

however, not in order to create new communities, like Frank Lloyd Wright's Taliesin or other rural utopias, but to find a voluntary and individual isolation in nature. Neruda, Erskine, Ernst, Malaparte, the Eameses, Lina Bo Bardi, O'Gorman, Bill and Ruth Lucas, Alison and Peter Smithson, all created a horizon of both escapism and self-reliance, trying to reconstruct the art of living from their own experiences, in the process of an endless reconstruction or self-construction of their daily lives.[19]

A historical reference to the fall of large social orders exists in Boccaccio's *Decameron,* which recounts the Black Death, the bubonic plague epidemic that devastated Europe in the mid-fourteenth century, breaking down all the civil and human bonds which maintained the good life of the medieval city. The lesson learned from the account in *The Decameron* is revealing: a young woman takes the initiative to convince six female friends and three young men to go away together to a country house outside of the city walls, so that they can protect themselves in the spirit of joy and humanity until the end of the plague. In the face of the fall of great orders, the art of reciprocal relationships can only begin from small orders. Neruda and Delia del Carril, the Erskines, the Eameses, the O'Gormans, the Smithsons and the Lucases also withdrew outside of the walls of the city to cabins of ephemeral appearance, where they tried to revive the bonds that permit to structure human life. Similarly to Boccaccio, they intuited that the new order of their lives would conform to a small scale: after daily life, after mutual human relationships, after nature, memories and imagination.

19 — Notions such as self-reliance and self-construction, which can be applied to some of the cases here described, are important in the American tradition that links the transcendentalism of Ralph Waldo Emerson to the pragmatism of John Dewey, passing through the poetics of Walt Whitman. The foundational work of this tradition of American thought is Emerson's master essay *Self-reliance*. See, Ralph Waldo Emerson, 'Self-reliance', in *Self-reliance and Other Essays* (New York: Dover, 1993), 19–38.

c. 1959

Finally, if I have chosen 1937 as a starting date, it is around 1959 when this emergence of dispersed and marginal self-experimentation begins to be institutionalized, leading to its own dissolution. In the same year, the reactive practices of Team X and their followers turned canonical, the CIAM disappeared and some of the values of continual experimentation were gradually transferred to the massive construction of contemporary architecture on the one hand, and to new groups of collective action on the other.[20] This was not only apparent in the architectural environment but it also occurred within the general trend that led to the emergence of new intellectual groups with new political and socio-cultural commitments. This socio-political reorganization reacting against the control of the two superpowers of the Cold War (the organization of the collective insurgencies that took place from the mid-1950s until their ultimate eruption during the events of May 1968) would bring with it also a reorientation of its responsive modes. As a consequence, these practices would no longer be oriented toward individual domestic self-experimentation in nature but rather toward proposals of new ideal communities and the recovery of the city for the public.

When opening up a topic such as domestic self-expression in nature, one cannot avoid the fact that we are involved in a recurring intellectual discussion in modern culture, a tradition that has a lot to do with the idea of the return to origins and its various incarnations. In the most general genealogy, this tradition could be traced back to Rousseau's *Emile ou l'education* (the work in which religiosity is wiped out from the myth of Robinson Crusoe in order to account for a secular list of a man's needs for nature),[21] passing through Henry-David Thoreau's *Walden* (already ripe with a romantic complex of guilt)[22] and culminating with Heidegger's cabin in Todtnauberg, where the philosopher laid the foundations for his metaphysical revolution beginning in 1923.[23] Spaces of refuge for an alternative experience that begin in the solitude of nature and that justify their beginning with a return to the origins are a part of the Enlightenment/Romantic

20 — The Team X Archives holding the documents for the organization of the last CIAM between 1957 and 1959 are quite significant to illustrate this shift. See TEAM X Archives, Harvard Graduate School of Design, Special Collections, Folder C016.

21 — 'In the natural order men are all equal, manhood is their common vocation; and anyone who is well trained for this vocation can not fulfil amiss any other which is related to it. It matters little to me whether my pupil be designed for the army, the church, or the bar. Nature has destined us to live as men. To live is the profession I would teach him. When I have done with him, it is true, he will be neither a lawyer, a soldier, nor a divine. He will first be a man; anything else that a man ought to be will become as occasion arises as soon as any other. Fortune may remove from rank to rank as she pleases, he will always be in his place.' Jean-Jacques Rousseau, *Emile, Julie and Other Writings* (New York: Barron's Educational Series, 1964), 63.

22 — Henry-David Thoreau's experience is described in the well-known book *Walden*. Henry-David Thoreau, *Walden, Or the Life in the Woods* (Boston: Ticknor and Fields, 1854).

23 — It might be interesting to see the work of Heidegger of this time and the key role of his cabin in the Black Forest. Rüdiger Safranski, *Martin Heidegger: Between Good and Evil* (Cambridge, MA: Harvard University Press, 1999), 129–43. See also Mark Wigley, 'Heidegger's House: The Violence of the Domestic', *Public* 6 (1992), 93–118.

Le Corbusier, Cabanon in Cap-Martin, 1952–65.
Photo: Francisco González de Canales.

tradition.[24] In architecture, the cabin proposed by Marc-Antoine Laugier, the ideological confirmation of the natural origin of architecture, would be paraphrased – yet with reservations – by Le Corbusier, as he reflected upon it in the works that opened and closed his career: from his designs of the house for a self-sufficient artisan to his own Cabanon in Cap Martin.[25] Nevertheless, this discussion is imbued with complexities and contradictions that deserve to be debated at more length.

Perhaps the work of Rousseau would be a suitable departure point for the previous genealogy, as it vividly represents the dramatic foundational conflict of modernity between the artificial and the natural. Rousseau with his social contract situated himself at a crossroad where, on the one hand, nature is the origin and the support, and on the other, the artificial and its pure geometries 'domesticate' the man and offer him the possibility of living in a social community.[26] For Rousseau, the man would be in the middle of a trajectory that goes from his biological origin to architecture that instructs and represents him, or as Georges Bataille pointed out with a critical irony: 'men seem to represent only an intermediary stage in the morphological process that goes from apes to great edifices'.[27] In reverse, architecture would be for a man what the cage is for an animal. Only from within this cage could the man contemplate nature; a cage from which to see, but not to touch – as from the large Corbusian windows – where any tactile excess, as much for Rousseau as for Thoreau, would be just pure degeneration.

However, while these *installations*[28] seem to respond to a Romantic/Enlightenment problem, for the man at the end of history, from whom the exterior has been confiscated, the situation is

24 — For more on this particular theme, it is interesting to check Peder Anker, 'The Philosopher's Cabin and the Household of Nature', in *Ethics, Place and Environment* 6.2 (June 2003), 131–141.

25 — A summary of this search for a primitive hut can be found in the Joseph Rykwert's canonical book *On Adam's House in Paradise. The Idea of the Primitive Hut in Architectural History* (New York: Museum of Modern Art; Chicago: Graham Foundation for Advanced Studies in the Fine Arts; Greenwich: New York Graphic Society, 1972). Regarding Le Corbusier, see his Complete Works, edited by him in 1956. Le Corbusier, *OEuvre complète* (Zúrich: Artemis, 1964).

26 — The implications of Rousseau's ideas on architecture have been discussed by Antohony Vidler in his studies of the architecture of the Enlightenment. Anthony Vidler, *The Writing of the Walls. Architecture Theory in the Late Enlightenment* (New York: Princeton Architectural Press, 1985), 23–44.

27 — George Bataille, "Architecture", in Neal Leach, ed., *Rethinking Architecture* (London and New York), 21. Translated by Paul Hagerty from the French original: *OEuvres complètes* (Paris: Gallimard, 1970–88).

28 — In the context of this book, I use the term 'installation' to reflect to a particular mode of settling, appropriating the Spanish notion of 'instalación'. In Spanish *instalación* is an especially charged word for architects. While it reflects the notion of an 'art installation', it also connotes a 'device' or an 'apparatus'. Simultaneously, it implies lightness, reversibility and even ephemerality.

totally different. For the Enlightened, Romantic and Modern man, nature was the other side. Nature objectified his exteriority – that is, the selfsame and most pure exterior – and as a consequence, it facilitated the definition of the man himself in dialectical terms, in which the man would be the pure interior. As a result of defining 'men' as a plurality of individual subjects, nature, the exterior, had to be defined as a singular object. In contrast, domestic self-experimentation does not have any possible exterior due to the paradoxical situation of the man at the end of history. Expropriated from the exterior that modern culture provided him with, the man of the end of history is forced to experiment with himself in order to create his own horizon of possibilities. However, it is also this particular circumstance that allows him to gather around a personal assembly of his own reality; in other words, to individually reorganize the now liberated human/nature relations.

The Conflicting Vernacular

Germán Rodríguez Arias and Pablo Neruda: Los Guindos, 1938–43, Isla Negra, 1943–56 and La Chascona, 1952–6, Chile

Pablo Neruda and his third wife Matilde Urrutia in front of the poet's house in Isla Negra c. 1956. Note that the tilted roof on the tower was consciously erased from the photograph by Germán Rodríguez Arias.
Photo: Germán Rodríguez Arias' professional archive. Historical Archive from the Col·legi d'Arquitectes de Catalunya, Barcelona.

I would like to thank Junta de Andalucía and Fundació La Caixa for sponsoring the research on which this chapter is based. I am also grateful to the Pablo Neruda Foundation, Delia del Carril Foundation, Catholic University of Chile School of Architecture in Santiago, University of Valparaiso School of Architecture, Harvard Graduate School of Design, University of Seville and Col·legi d'Arquitectes de Catalunya for their institutional support. I am also indebted to many individuals for their comments on this work and their help with particular materials: Nuria Álvarez Lombardero, Sibel Bozdogan, Raul Bulnes, Luis E. Carranza, Carlos Durán, Barbara Elfman, Adrian Gorelik, K. Michael Hays, Mirta Halpert, Felipe Hernández, Juan José Lahuerta, Carlos Martnel, José Ramón Moreno, Luis Moreno Mansilla, J. Rafael Moneo, Hernán Montesinos, Fernando Pérez Oyarzun, Ignacio Quintana, Fernando Saenz, Hashim Sarkis, Graciela Silvestri, Sergio Soza, Eduardo Subirats, Horacio Torrent and Emilio Tuñón. I would like to extend my gratitude to George Dodds for his patience and guidance.

In 1957 Catalan architect Germán Rodríguez Arias carefully erased the tower roof and some other additions that the poet Pablo Neruda had made to Rodríguez Arias's original design for the poet's house in Isla Negra **[see page before]**.[1] This event marked the end of a long and contentious relationship between the poet laureate and the modernist architect responsible for the design of three famous houses in which Neruda lived **[figures 1 and 2]**. Designed between 1943 and 1956, the three houses remain not only a legacy of the turbulent partnership between the poet and the architect but are also notable for embodying two opposing understandings of the cultural legacy of Republican Spain and its strong bond of the avant-garde with vernacular and popular culture, that had been intensely experienced by both men before the three houses were built.[2]

Before his exile to Chile in 1939, Rodríguez Arias was one of the founders and most representative architects of the *Grup d'Artistes i Tècnics Catalans per al Progrés de l'Arquitectura Contemporània*

1 — Pablo Neruda was born in Parral, Chile, in 1904, and died in Santiago de Chile on September 23, 1973. With works that have been translated into more than twenty languages, Neruda is one of the most influential and best-known poets of the twentieth century. He held several diplomatic positions, including that of a consul in Madrid under Republican Spain (1934–1937). From the Spanish Civil War onwards, his political activism paralleled his poetry. In 1971 he received the Nobel Prize for Literature. According to the literary critic Alistair Reid, 'Neruda is the most widely read poet since William Shakespeare'.

2 — Between 1931 and 1937, during the Second Republic, Spain underwent a cultural revolution. People like Federico García Lorca, Joan Miró or Luis Buñuel belonged to a new generation of artists who were also important intellectual and social activists. Both Neruda and Rodríguez Arias lived through this period and had to leave the country during the Spanish Civil War (1936–9).

[Figure 1] Interior of Los Guindos house, La Reina, Santiago de Chile, 1943–5. The living room features some of the Ibiza-inspired furniture designed by Rodríguez Arias for Muebles Sur, the company that he founded in 1942 along with two other Catalan exiles, Claudio Tarragó and Cristian Aguadé. ***Arquitectura y construcción*** **magazine #10. Publisher: Zig-zag, September 1974. Courtesy of Carlos Durán.**

[Figure 2] Germán Rodríguez Arias and Pablo Neruda, La Chascona house, Bellavista, Santiago de Chile, 1952–6. Green ceramic floors, rough wood and coloured glass create highly sensual and slightly kitschy atmosphere typical of Neruda's houses. **Photo: Nuria Álvarez Lombardero.**

(GATCPAC), a group of modernist architects led by Josep Lluís Sert, who was very active in Spain during the 1930s.[3] Rodríguez Arias's designs for Isla Negra, Los Guindos and La Chascona are among the few works of the GATCPAC architects realized after the 1930s, with the exception of the more international and well-known case of Josep Lluís Sert in the United States. Despite their apparent singularity, Rodríguez Arias's houses as a trio can be analysed in a way that enriches our understanding of GATCPAC's modern vernacular agenda, and how in Chile they tested its possible extension to other countries.

Neruda's insistent alterations developed from a tentative critique to a deliberate counter-agenda to Rodríguez Arias's architectural project. After he had moved into his new homes, Neruda modified, changed and constantly expanded them, tracing speculative trajectories of new spatial practices. Conscious of the symbolic value of 'the house of the poet', he used each of these constructions as a laboratory in which he could explore the evocative power of material sensations as a parallel to his poetic ambitions. Neruda's own spatial arrangements and experiments propose an alternative response to the anxieties of vernacular modernism, reassembling in different ways the specificity of any cultural and material presence as a part of the daily experience of inhabiting. This chapter assesses these two attitudes evinced in the three houses and elaborates on the appropriation of vernacular and popular references in the practices of the modernist architectural culture of Spain of the 1930s.

3 — The *Grup d'Artistes i Tecnics Catalans per al Progrès de l'Arquitectura Contemporània* (GATCPAC) is the Catalan branch of the three organizations that comprised the *Grupo de Artistas y Técnicos Españoles para el Progreso de la Arquitectura Contemporánea* (GATEPAC), the Association of Spanish Modern Architects active in Spain between 1930 and 1937, recognized as the official Spanish delegation of the *Comité International pour la Résolution des Problèmes de l'Architecture Contemporaine* (CIRPAC) since 1932. The GATCPAC was the only branch of the GATEPAC that worked as a group, producing some notable works. The most remarkable architects of this group were Sixt Illescas, Germán Rodríguez Arias, Josep Lluís Sert, Josep Maria Subirana, Josep Torres-Clavé or the future architect Antonio Bonet. For further information see Antonio Pizza and Josep M. Rovira (eds.), *GATCPAC: A New Architecture for a New City: 1928–1939* (Barcelona: Col·legi d'Arquitectes de Catalunya, 2006).

The Architect

By the early 1930s GATCPAC epitomised the centre of modernist architecture in Spain. However, the group's work did not reach maturity until the mid-1930s and the first works by the Catalan architects not very reflectively appropriated certain features of their chosen Northern European models. A close look at *A. C. Documentos de Actividad Contemporánea*, the group's official publication, edited in Barcelona between 1932 and 1937, confirms this assertion.[4] Images of the work of Josep Lluís Sert and Germán Rodríguez Arias are juxtaposed with the work of modernist architects such as J. P. P. Oud, as if through superficial similarities one could assert the validity of the Spanish designs. Germán Rodríguez Arias's first creations in Barcelona were also influenced by the desire to resemble the language of the works by the canonical European modernists. Buildings such as his apartments at 61 Vía Augusta (Barcelona, 1930), the façade of which seems to correspond to a fully modernist building, are organized according to the typical plan of the nineteenth-century block in Barcelona, separated by rigid structural walls **[figure 3]**. The same applies to another celebrated design by Rodríguez Arias from this period: the Astoria building (Barcelona, 1932), constructed around tiny interior patios.

Supported by the Republican Government of Catalonia, the group became involved in education, health and public housing programmes. In buildings such as the Anti-Tuberculosis Day Clinic (Barcelona, 1935) and the Casa Bloc Housing (Barcelona, 1935) by Sert, Subirana and Torres Clavé, GATCPAC revealed the social implications of modern architecture that had been missing in its previous modernist practices. The strengthening of GATCPAC's ideological discourse, however, came about through its association with Le Corbusier, who had been in contact with some architects of the group as early as 1928.[5] GATCPAC communicated with Le Corbusier when the modern master was undergoing a shift from the *machine à habiter* towards an architecture that made allusions to local cultures.[6] Constricted by Le Corbusier's

4 — Although the GATCPAC was mainly responsible for the publication, *A. C. (Documentos de Actividad Contemporánea)* represented the entire GATEPAC group. It was a typical avant-garde magazine like *ABC*, *G* or *De Stijl*, with very strong statements and not so much self-criticism. The directors of the magazine were Josep Lluís Sert and his partner Josep Torres-Clavé. The entire collection of A. C. issues was reprinted as a facsimile in Barcelona in 2005: *AC Publicación del GATEPAC* (Barcelona: Fundación Caja de Arquitectos, 2005).

5 — Josep Lluís Sert met Le Corbusier in Madrid 1928, when the Swiss architect came to Spain for the first time to lecture at the Residencia de Estudiantes. By then, Sert had persuaded Le Corbusier to repeat the same lectures in Barcelona, starting a strong relationship, first as a disciple and collaborator in Le Corbusier's office, and later, as a loyal friend. The fruit of this relationship between Le Corbusier and Sert was the collaboration between the GATCPAC and Le Corbusier, with remarkable examples such as the Plan Macià for Barcelona (1932–34) or the re-adaptation of a housing block in L'Eixample, Barcelona (1933).

6 — After his failures in the Palace of the League of Nations and the Palace of Soviets, and his diminishing influence in the CIAM discourse – by then dominated by the Germans – Le Corbusier began to reshape his position developing sympathies with the French trade unionists' ideology, exuberance of the Latin American

ideological apparatus, GATCPAC became a direct inheritor to this revised modernist agenda and turn to the vernacular.[7] Hence, in the essays and speeches of the Catalan group, the metaphor of *the Mediterranean* – also used by Le Corbusier – would become a powerful point of reference.[8] In the metaphor of the Mediterranean culture GATCPAC found the origin of a modern architect's two major preoccupations: the recovery of the classical (universal values) and the engagement with the popular (the people), or in other words, the simultaneous production of objectivity (the machine) and subjectivity (the emotion).

GATCPAC's major effort was to prove the natural convergence between the modern and the popular/vernacular in the Mediterranean context. This was accomplished in numerous articles on the links between modernism and Mediterranean popular culture published in the *A. C.* journal. A paradigmatic example is *A. C.* 21, a special issue dedicated to popular architecture in Ibiza. This topic had already been introduced in *A. C.* 6, featuring the article 'Ibiza: The Island that Does Not Need Architectural Renovation', attributed to Germán Rodríguez Arias.[9] Dozens of pictures of Ibiza's vernacular architecture supported the architect's argument that the Mediterranean popular architecture was 'modern by nature', 'rational in essence' and 'wise in its construction methods'. [figure 4] Following this panegyric, the referential images from high modernism were combined with a more modest, semi-rustic sensibility, and the mechanical skeletons of GATCPAC's architecture were suddenly filled with country décor, rural furniture, ceramic floors and traditional Mediterranean household goods, such as drinking jugs and artisanal wine bottles.

countries, primitivism closely related to some contemporary French surrealist trends and vindication of certain vernacular values common to all of them. Exemplary designs manifesting this ideological shift are Villa Errázuriz (1929–30), Villa Mandrot (1930) and villa in Les Mathes (1935). An introduction to Le Corbusier's vernacular shift can be found in: Francesco Passanti, 'The Vernacular, Modernism, and Le Corbusier', *The Journal of the Society of Architectural Historians*, 56.4 (1997), 438–451.

7 — The influence of Le Corbusier is very present in other cases of modernist engagement with the vernacular in the 1930s. For instance, it would be highly interesting to compare GATCPAC with a prominent case of Brazilian modernism. For a compelling reflection on Brazilian modernist culture see Fernando Luiz Lara, 'Modernism Made Vernacular: The Brazilian case', *Journal of Architectural Education*, 63,1 (2009), 41–50.

8 — Antonio Pizza, 'The Mediterranean: Creation and Development of a Myth', in *Josep Lluís Sert and the Mediterranean* (Barcelona: Col·legi d'Arquitectes de Catalunya, 1996), 14–45. Some very eloquent speeches by Sert and Rodríguez Arias are published in this book and give a sense of this ideological position.

9 — The topic of *A. C.* 18 was 'The Popular Mediterranean Architecture' (*La arquitectura popular mediterránea*), while *A. C.* 21 was more precisely on 'Popular Architecture in Ibiza' (*Arquitectura popular en Ibiza*). *A. C.* 21 appeared with two long untitled articles signed by Raoul Haussman and Erwin Heilbronner. Raoul Haussman, 'Untitled', *A. C. Documentos de la actividad contemporánea* 21 (1935), 11–24 and Erwin Heilbronner, 'Untitled', *A. C. Documentos de la actividad contemporánea* 21 (1935), 15–23. See also Germán Rodríguez Arias, 'Ibiza, la isla que no necesita renovación arquitectónica', *A. C. Documentos de la actividad contemporánea* 6 (1932), 28–30.

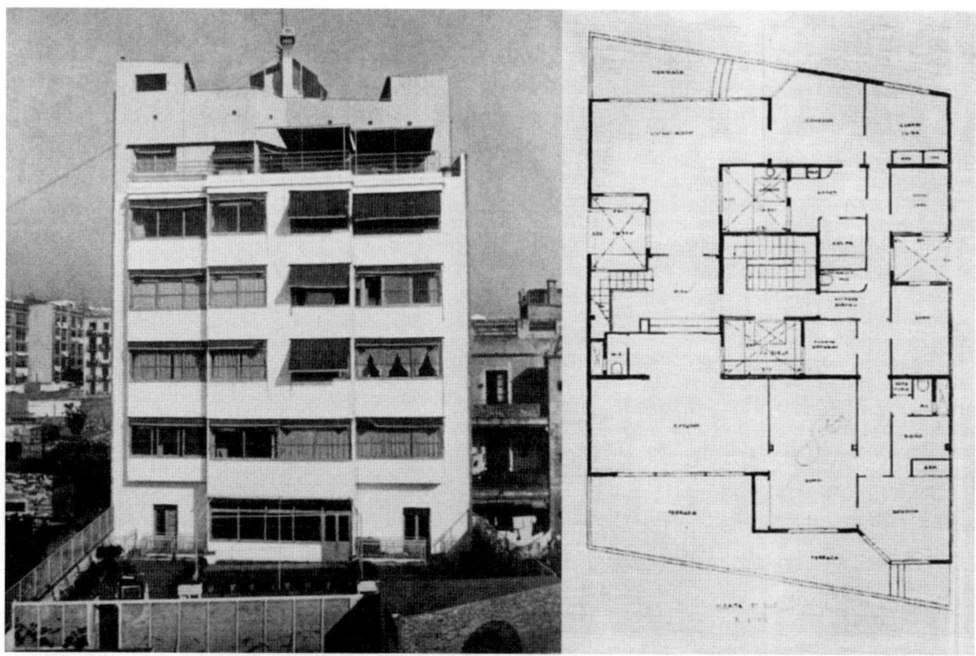

[Figure 3] Germán Rodríguez Arias, housing at 61 Vía Augusta, Barcelona, 1931. The image of the façade as published in published in A. C. 8 (1932) and the anti-modernist floor plan from Rodríguez Arias´s professional archives that he never wanted to publish. ***A .C. Documentos de Acción Contemporánea* and Germán Rodriguez Arias Professional Archive. Historical Archive of the Col·legi d'Arquitectes de Catalunya, Barcelona.**

[Figure 4] Vernacular architecture in Ibiza, from the article 'Ibiza: The Island that Does Not Need Architectural Renovation', *A. C.* 6 (1932). Note that the tilted roofs on some of the constructions were also erased by Rodríguez Arias. The image of the vernacular is fixed as a universal elemental geometry. ***A .C. Documentos de Acción Contemporánea*** **and Germán Rodriguez Arias Professional Archive. Historical Archive of the Col·legi d'Arquitectes de Catalunya, Barcelona.**

[Figure 5] Germán Rodríguez Arias, House in San Antonio, Ibiza, 1935, as published in *A. C.* 19 (1935). The building epitomizes Rodríguez Arias's belief in modern architecture based on the model of vernacular Mediterranean architecture. ***A .C. Documentos de Acción Contemporánea*** **and Germán Rodriguez Arias Professional Archive. Historical Archive of the Col·legi d'Arquitectes de Catalunya, Barcelona.**

[Figure 6] Interior of Germán Rodríguez Arias's house in San Antonio, Ibiza, 1935, showing the typical atmosphere of a traditional Ibizan house. ***A .C. Documentos de Acción Contemporánea*** **and Germán Rodriguez Arias Professional Archive. Historical Archive of the Col·legi d'Arquitectes de Catalunya, Barcelona.**

Germán Rodríguez Arias's most extreme example built following this ideological prescription is the house that he designed in San Pedro, Ibiza, in 1935. Unlike the most refined houses in Garraf, Catalonia, by Josep Lluís Sert and Josep Torres Clavé that were built in the same period, the architect's belief in the Mediterranean paradigm was so compelling that it was difficult to differentiate the San Pedro house from any other vernacular houses. Extremely modest and rigorous, both in material and type, the house advocates a modernist tradition that is deeply rooted in a particular local culture. Indeed, it is difficult to see anything 'modern' about it. The centralized plan, the harshness and rusticity of the materials and the simplicity of the traditional construction do not incorporate any of the typical modernist features, from either a technical, spatial or social point of view. The interior of the house reflects the lifestyle of an ordinary Ibizan family, following the same customs that the islanders have practiced for decades **[figures 5 and 6]**. Rodríguez Arias justified the modernity of his construction in the frank openness of the house towards the exterior, deploying generous terraces towards the sun, and a quite rational use of materials and spatial distribution. He would consider anything beyond this austere architecture as a weak rhetoric of his first years of engagement with modernist architecture – the rhetoric to be left behind.[10]

Perhaps the most sincere believer in the Mediterranean cause of the entire group, Rodríguez Arias would bring his convictions into exile in Chile. However, his Mediterranean architecture never seemed to take root in the American soil. The skirting boards of limestone, simple white volumes and wide open terraces would be mirrored upside down in Chile: as dark and rounded stones, complexly articulated volumes and sheltered dwelling domains. It is remarkable to highlight how Rodríguez Arias's preliminary proposal for the Isla Negra house displays a large terrace facing the ocean, one that would be never used because of Chile's constant chilly winds from the West.[11] Transferred to the Pacific, Rodríguez Arias's Mediterranean venture would be like a shore without an

10 — 'Casa en San Antonio, Ibiza', *A. C. Documentos de la actividad contemporánea* 19, (1935).

11 — Pilar Calderón and Marc Folch, Neruda–Rodríguez Arias. *Cases per a un poeta / Casas para un poeta / Houses for a poet* (Barcelona: Col·legi d'Arquitectes de Catalunya, 2004), 41.

ocean, an architectural agenda ultimately rejected by the Chilean poet.[12]

The Architect and the Poet

The three houses that Pablo Neruda commissioned Germán Rodríguez Arias to design have distinct histories. The oldest, Los Guindos, is a restoration of a colonial house in the commune of La Reina, acquired by Neruda when he arrived from Spain with Delia del Carril in 1938. Rodríguez Arias restored it around 1943, preserving the exterior while refurbishing the interior [figure 7]. He installed large glass walls facing the yard, where Neruda placed a small theatre dedicated to his late friend, Federico García Lorca [figures 8 and 9]. In the yard and around the theatre, the poet organized his famous *asados* (barbecue parties), which would earn him the reputation of a *bon vivant*. If Los Guindos was the house for parties and get-togethers, Isla Negra was the place for solitude and reflection. Neruda purchased the house from the Spanish sailor Eladio Sobrino when it was nothing but a stone cottage [figure 10]. Rodríguez Arias restored and expanded it between 1943 and 1945. Later, it was further altered by Neruda himself with the assistance of the local architect Sergio Soza.[13] Above all, Isla Negra was the place to write, and was probably the most representative of the poet's houses [figures 11 and 12]. Finally, Neruda commissioned Rodríguez Arias to build the third house, La Chascona, as the home that Neruda would share with Matilde Urrutia after his split from Delia del Carril. Neruda later expanded it with the help of the architect Carlos Martnel. In contrast to Los Guindos and Isla Negra, La Chascona has a multinuclear configuration, comprising three separate detached constructions: the living room, dining room and library, all with bedrooms attached in different ways [figure 13].[14]

12 — A more extensive reflection on the work of Rodríguez Arias in Chile can be found in: Francisco González de Canales, 'Stone on Stone: Germán Rodríguez Arias Andean Architecture', in *ARQ* 71 (2009), 80–3.

13 — According to Elena Mayorga, although the shareholders' agreement was signed in 1939, it seems that Neruda made a deal with Eladio Sobrino around 1938, or even earlier. The house that Neruda bought was designed by Eladio's daughter Luz Sobrino, who was then an architecture student. Elena Mayorga, *Las casas de Pablo Neruda* (Diploma thesis, Universidad del Bío-Bío, 1996), 77–79.

13 — There are documents of Germán Rodríguez Arias's first project at the Col·legi d'Arquitectes de Catalunya, including floor plans, sketches and a blueprint for a second extension, which was not built. Minor additions were made by Neruda with the help of a local mason, Rafita. Following Rodríguez Arias's departure to Spain in 1956, Sergio Soza became the architect in charge of later extensions of Isla Negra. However, Sergio Soza recognizes that he was acting just as a technical assistant for Neruda's own designs. Segio Soza in an interview by the author, Santiago de Chile (March 16, 2005).

14 — These three houses are not the only ones Neruda had. He later built La Sebastiana in Valparaíso. Toward the end of his life, Neruda bought land and commissioned another house in Santiago, La Manquel. The young architect Ramiro Insuza was commissioned, but the house was never built because of Neruda's death.

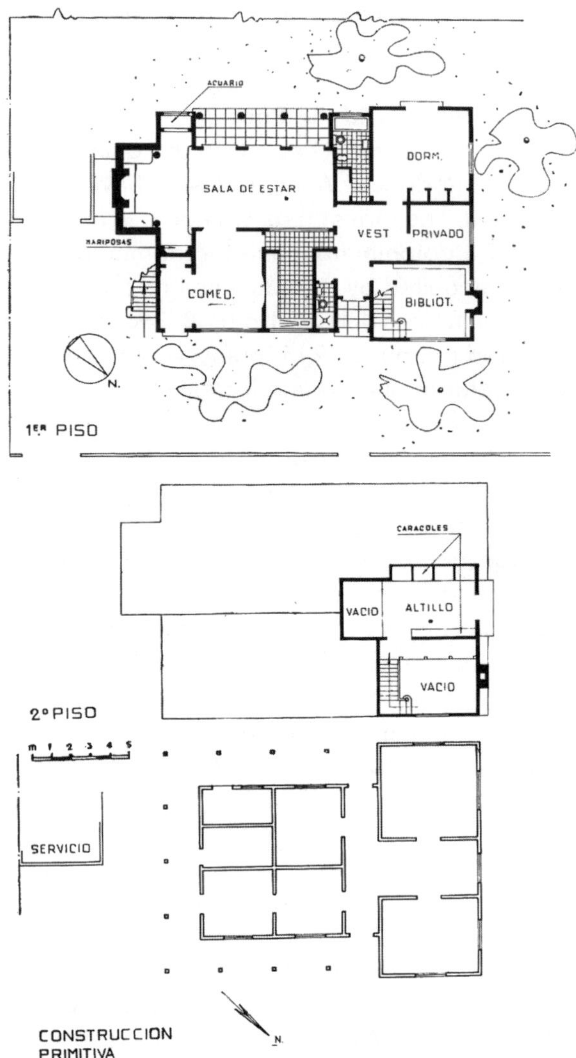

[Figure 7] Rodríguez Arias, renovation of Los Guindos, house plan, c.1943. An interesting architectural promenade articulates two different levels of the house, using the library and two-storey living room as main connectors. The promenade regulates the transition from the occlusion of the main façade to the wide openings towards the back yard. ***Arquitectura y construcción* magazine #10. Publisher: Zig-zag. September 1974. Courtesy of Carlos Durán.**

[Figure 8] Rodríguez Arias, Los Guindos, c. 1945. Glass wall in the living room framing the Araucaria, the tree under which Neruda used to write his poems. **Germán Rodriguez Arias' Professional Archive. Historical Archive of the Col·legi d'Arquitectes de Catalunya, Barcelona.**

[Figure 9] Rodríguez Arias, Los Guindos. Federico García Lorca theatre, c. 1945. The theatre functioned also as a barbecue space for Neruda's gatherings in Santiago. This precarious shed looks like a timber version of Rodríguez Arias's Ibizan architecture, with its flat roofs, small windows, external stairs, heavy stone baseboards, elemental geometries, etc. Two enormous tree trunks found by Neruda on site frame the stage as the poet had asked the architect to integrate them into the architectural design. **Germán Rodriguez Arias' Professional Archive. Historical Archive of the Col·legi d'Arquitectes de Catalunya, Barcelona.**

[Figure 10] Isla Negra house before Rodríguez Arias's renovation, c. 1938.
Photo: Pablo Neruda's Foundation Archive, Santiago de Chile.

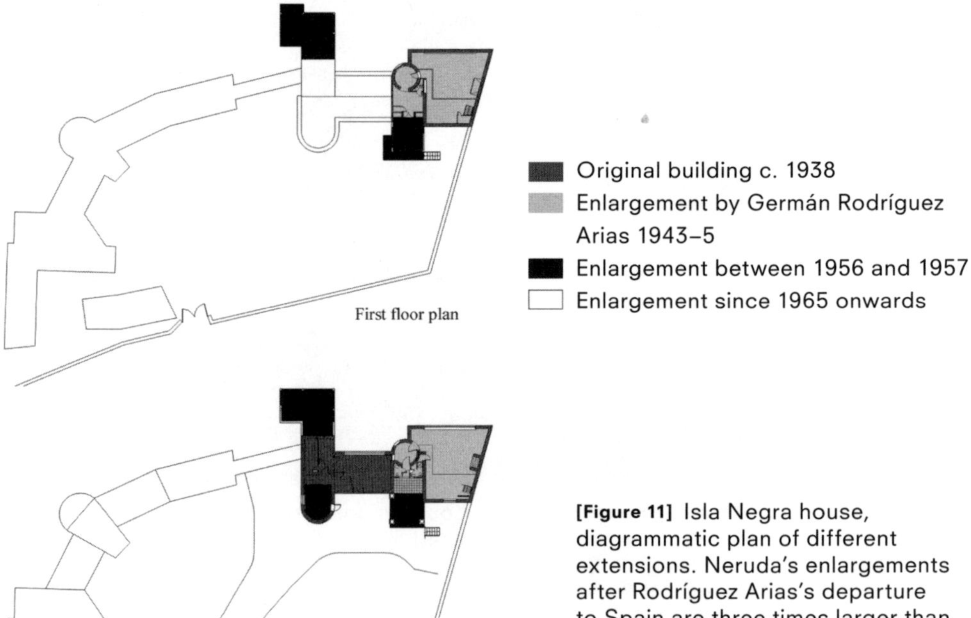

First floor plan

- Original building c. 1938
- Enlargement by Germán Rodríguez Arias 1943–5
- Enlargement between 1956 and 1957
- Enlargement since 1965 onwards

[Figure 11] Isla Negra house, diagrammatic plan of different extensions. Neruda's enlargements after Rodríguez Arias's departure to Spain are three times larger than the one designed by the architect. **Drawings: Francisco González de Canales and Nuria Álvarez Lombardero.**

[Figure 12] View of the Isla Negra house with some of the extensions made by Neruda. **Photo: Luis Poirot.**

[Figure 13] Exterior view of La Chascona, 1956. According to Rodríguez Arias, the design of this multinuclear house is the work of Pablo Neruda. **Photo: Luis Poirot.**

These three houses also show the multifariousness of the relationship between the architect and the poet. In Los Guindos and Isla Negra, Neruda gives Rodríguez Arias a basic programme and set of ideas that the Spaniard has to channel through the principles of the GATCPAC, which he used in his designs for the houses in Ibiza at the beginning of the 1930s. In short, these two constructions respond to the spatial organization of Le Corbusier's Pavillion de L'Esprit Nouveau, built for the 1925 Art Deco exhibition in Paris: the *promenade architecturale*, two-storey living room and *fenêtre à longer*.[15] Moreover, they incorporate some of the vernacular imagery that Le Corbusier had been putting into practice since his Errázuriz house (1930), designed for a site in Chile. The Errázuriz house proves an extremely important reference to the development of the ideas displayed in the Isla Negra house by Rodríguez Arias, specifically in the relation to its surroundings. In the Errázuriz house the roofs are sloped to maintain a visual continuity with the ascent of the mountains and this movement is incorporated into the house through the interior ramps. This *promenade architecturale,* seemingly an intentional mimesis of the ascent of the local mountain slopes, also directs us to the master bedroom, the most private space of the house. Below, an enormous window draws the eye to the immensity of the ocean. In the Errázuriz house the landscape slips into the house, bringing a new meaning to the spatial configurations of its interior. With a similar structure the house at Isla Negra can be read as the ascent over the ocean horizon, rising over the rock that Neruda welcomed into his living room, continuing to the tower, the most private place, where the bedroom is located **[figure 14 and 15]**. This architectural promenade that spatially structures the house is limited not only to its internal organization but also to a conscious register of the existing landscape and its material presence, evinced in the sustained tension between the cliff and the ocean. The material vernacular look of the Errázuriz house is also present in Isla Negra. However,

15 — This pavilion, which was a 1 to 1 scale prototype of Le Corbusier's housing unit for his Immeuble-Villa, had an enormous impact on early modern Spanish architects. Impressed by their visit to the Art Deco Exhibition in Paris, this first group of modern architects in Spain, including Carlos Arniches, Rafael Bergamín, Martín Domínguez, Casto Fernández Shaw, Fernando García Mercadal, Luis Lacasa and Manuel Santos Arcas, received the name of *Generación del 25* (1925 generation). See Sofía Diéguez Patao, *La generación del 25. Primera arquitectura moderna en Madrid* (Madrid: Cátedra, 1997).

[Figure 14] Interior of the living room at Isla Negra as designed by Rodríguez Arias between 1943 and 1945. The architectural promenade which structures the architect's intervention departs from the ribbon window facing the ocean and goes over the natural rock that Neruda wanted to leave inside the living room. The promenade continues parallel to the perimeter of the two-storey living room, passing through the private library and ultimately reaching the small bedroom hidden at the top of the tower. In the image, Neruda's collection of figureheads starts to take over Rodríguez Arias's spatial structure. **Photo: Luis Poirot.**

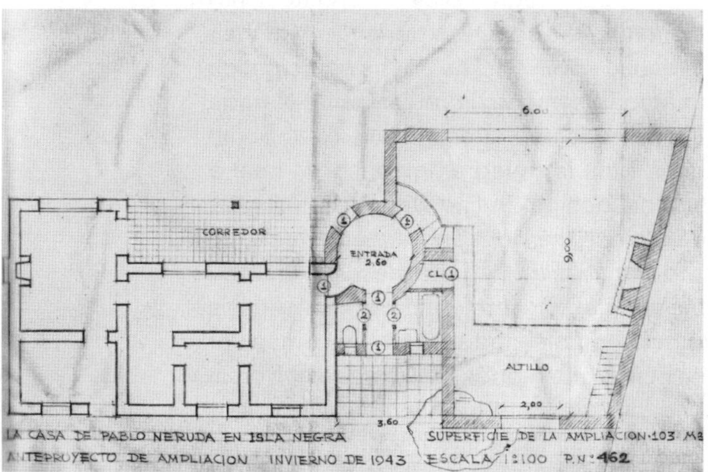

[Figure 15] Plan of Rodríguez Arias's extension for Isla Negra, where the main elements of the architectural promenade proposed by the Catalan are also visible: the ribbon window, rock, mezzanine of the private library and small bedroom inside the tower. The open terrace connecting the extension with the original construction is one of the Mediterranean features which would never work in the Chilean context as it faces strong winds from the ocean. **Germán Rodriguez Arias' Professional Archive. Historical Archive of the Col·legi d'Arquitectes de Catalunya, Barcelona.**

while Le Corbusier rejected the logic of vernacular construction and treated this house and others (such as his Villa Mandrot or house in Les Mathes) with the same smooth, uniform and continuous surface of his first purist houses, though now tinted with a vernacular texture, Rodríguez Arias seemed to be truer to the vernacular logic. In Isla Negra the stone wall is not just a texture applied to an abstract continuous wall but a careful assemblage of materials – an expression of aesthetic effect congruent with its logic of construction.

Rodríguez Arias's designs for Los Guindos and Isla Negra had organized a strong architectural system around architectural promenades linking the interior and exterior of the houses, which were later modified by appropriating different materials specific to the site and the poet's belongings. Particularities such as the view of the ocean, an enormous rock in the middle of the property, gigantic tree trunk found nearby, stones from the shore, as well as personal touches like a stone tower, a particular kind of window and an important number of specific objects from the poet's personal collections, are correctly integrated by the architect into the building structure, animating the spatial experience with their material and referential presence **[figure 16]**. The poet's participation in the selection of the material elements is remarkable; Neruda even sketched them with his trademark green ink **[figure 17]**. Some of his drawings, as those for the Isla Negra house show, bear a filial resemblance to the final design. In line with the principles established in dialogue between the poet and the architect, the task of the designer was to diacritically integrate these cultural and material elements into the architectural project. Rodríguez Arias's belief in the relationship between the modern and the vernacular as two sides of the same coin – one responsible for the universal logic of spatial structuring and the other for the material expression of the quotidian – allowed him to satisfy the poet's desires. However, once the architect completed the construction, the relationship between architecture and material expression became fixed and unmovable. The rock entering the living room is now anchored there, so are the wood trunks comprising the passable

[Figure 16] Sketch by Rodríguez Arias trying to integrate different materials brought by the poet Neruda to the project, such as pots, bottles, shells, maps, and other objects. **Pablo Neruda's Foundation Archive, Santiago de Chile.**

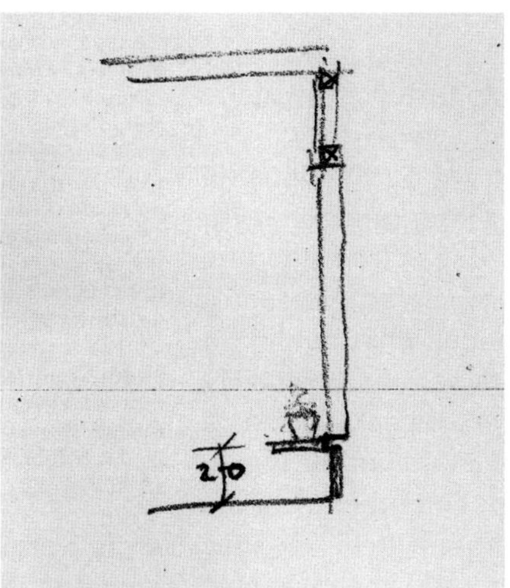

awnings, and so are the stones in the walls. All the unexpected conjunctions of different material realities are frozen in time and space, preventing any further manipulation or any interactions different from the ones the architect had chosen.

Neruda's reaction to this architectural stasis was almost immediate. It is said that while Rodríguez Arias was still finishing the construction, the poet, already living in the houses, began modifying them. An inverse relationship developed: the further away the architect was from the house, the more ambitious were Neruda's modifications. The poet altered the criteria imposed by the architect, creating new atmospheres, changing the purpose of some rooms, giving meaning to spaces through the objects he displayed in them and even modelling the interiors through the use of these very objects. This approach to spatial production is clearly present in the last house that Rodríguez Arias designed for the poet, La Chascona. That is why, when La Chascona was finished in 1956, Rodríguez Arias – who claimed that he had merely participated as a technician – was able to state: 'This isn't mine anymore. This is a house designed by Pablo.'[16]

The Poet

From 1946 on, Neruda began to take charge of the design and construction, increasing his disconnection from the architect.[17] The second expansion that Neruda commissioned to Rodríguez Arias for Isla Negra was never built – at least, not the one that the architect had designed. In fact, Neruda's experience in manipulating spaces while settling in Isla Negra and Los Guindos raised the possibility of deploying his own spatial practices. It appears that he needed only the help of Rafita (an Isla Negra mason) or some local architects as technical assistants, who would never tamper with his designs. Sergio Soza, one of these architects, described himself as nothing more than the 'editor of Neruda's poetic of space'.[18]

16 — Matilde Urrutia, *My Life with Pablo Neruda*, trans. Alexandria Giardino (Stanford: Stanford University Press, 1996), 176. Matilde adds: 'Neruda changed the architectural plans every day; he modified the details, and ends to remind the living with an only wall, all the rest windows. He discussed with Germán over and over again.'

17 — Elena Mayorga has registered different independent plans by Pablo Neruda to extend Isla Negra after Rodríguez Arias's second expansion (1945) was never realized. Mayorga, *Las casas de Pablo Neruda*, 86–84.

18 — Segio Soza in an interview by the author (March 16, 2005). Soza was the architect for Isla Negra from 1957 on. Carlos Martnel, the architect who worked for Neruda in La Chascona after Rodríguez Arias's departure, declared that he never influenced Neruda's design. Carlos Martnel in an interview by the author, Santiago de Chile (March 23, 2005).

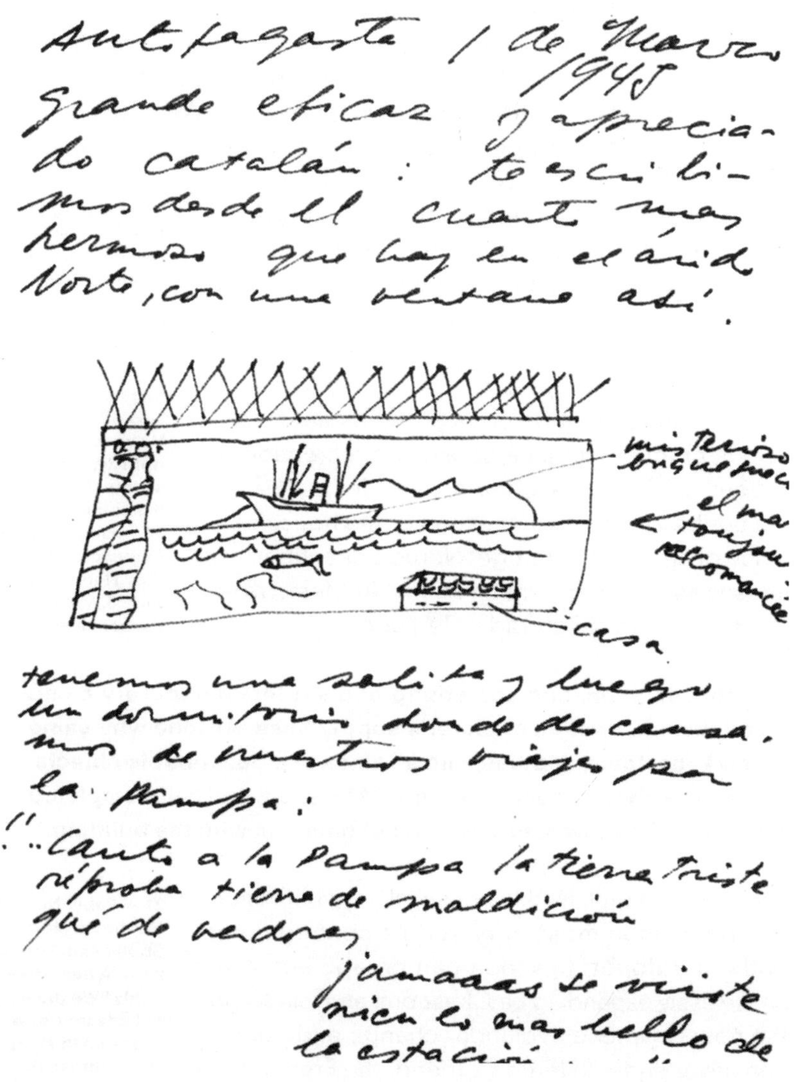
Antofagasta 1 de Marzo
1945
Grande eficaz y apreciado catalán: te escribimos desde el cuarto más hermoso que hay en el árido Norte, con una ventana así.

tenemos una salita y luego un dormitorio donde descansamos de nuestros viajes por la Pampa:
"..Canto a la Pampa la tierra triste réproba tierra de maldición qué de verdores
jamaaas se viste ni en lo más bello de la estación .."

[Figure 17] Drawing for Isla Negra house by Pablo Neruda, found in a letter addressed to Rodríguez Arias in 1945. The drawing depicts the poet's idea for his living room window. Neruda called it his 'Oceanic Window'. **Germán Rodriguez Arias' Professional Archive. Historical Archive of the Col·legi d'Arquitectes de Catalunya, Barcelona.**

Neruda's spatial practices were not unconscious. Not only did he know the symbolic value of houses such as Isla Negra, but he also had an enormous interest in architecture and construction in general. That is why, when asked what he would like to be in his life aside from being a poet, he answered: 'Builder, I would build houses'.[19] According to Neruda, there is a parallel between architecture and poetry: 'when making poetry and when making houses, there is always something that is sprouting, growing; ... building implies the sensuality of wood, varnishes, colours and objects, that are recognized and displayed with an architectural purpose'.[20] Therefore, Neruda's architecture cannot be considered as an unconscious practice but as a conscious recreation of spaces, and material effects and affects.

In contrast to most definitions of the house as a place of shelter and refuge, Neruda describes his houses as precarious installations. In *Memoirs* he remembers his childhood in Temuco:

19 — 'My biggest pleasure is the construction.' Raúl Mellado, 'Neruda responde a 23 Preguntas de El Siglo – Homenaje a los 60 años de Neruda', *Diario el Siglo*, July 12, 1964; 'If you had not chosen poetry as a way of life, would you have wanted to be a teacher? – Neruda: I would have been a builder. I would build houses.' Luis Alberto Ganderats, 'Neruda a lo Humano y a lo Poético', *El Mercurio*, April 20, 1969. Unless otherwise noted, all translations from Spanish are by the author.

20 — Emilio Filippi, Julio Lanzarotti, Augusto Olivares and Carlos Jonquera, 'Con Neruda en el 9', *Diario el Siglo*, July 13, 1969 (from an interview in Canal 9 television).

Our houses, then, had something of a settlers' temporary camp about them ... or of an explorer's supply base. Anyone who came in saw kegs, tools, saddles, and all kinds of indescribable objects. There were always rooms that weren't finished, and half-completed stairways. There was, forever, talk of going on with the building.[21]

This idea of a ramshackle house, always unfinished, can be seen in most of Neruda's constructions. Without a doubt, this idea can be applied to the ceaselessly expanding La Chascona and Isla Negra, the houses whose evolution, change and adaptation never ended. Neruda's friend, the French poet Louis Aragon, describes Isla Negra as 'a home like a shuffled house of cards' – a house that finds its own sense after an earthquake as if it knew its own fate.[22] Thus – following different metaphors for the risky,

21 — Pablo Neruda, *Memoirs*, trans. Hardie St. Martin (New York: Farrar, Straus and Giroux, 2003), 9.

22 — 'A home like a shuffled house of cards/ We did not read more fortune but adventure/ A house made of seaweed to sleep at future/ A house like a phrase that says you'. Louis Aragon, *Élégie à Pablo Neruda* (Paris: Gallimard, 1966), 16. The poem was born after the partial destruction of the Isla Negra in the earthquake of 1965. According to Aragon, the earthquake gives true meaning to the house.

open and provisional – poetry and dwelling grew together as the Isla Negra and Neruda's best-known poem, *Canto General*, developed simultaneously for more than a decade.[23]

Yet, the sensibility which governed Neruda's material expression stemmed mainly from his recovery of the sensual world, that occurred when he encountered Spanish poets in Madrid in the mid-1930s. When he met Federico García Lorca, *Three Material Songs* emerged, and with it a new poetry that shifted his production from the cold intellectual modernism of the first *Residence on Earth* to the engagement with the sensuality of material life.[24] This recuperation which had evolved in his poetry culminated in *Canto General*, the epic poem he began when he started to build Isla Negra. From that moment on, both the house and the poetry would be interwoven as a twofold material expression – the house as yet another 'material song'. This expression can be apprehended in the palpability of 'Entrance into Wood', the first of *Three Material Songs*, where the exacerbation of the materiality of the wood acquires 'mystical' properties:

23 — In *Canto General* Neruda remembers the same sensitivity in a poetic evocation: 'My house, the walls whose fresh,/ recently cut wood still smells: dilapidated/ homestead that creaked/ with every step, and whistled with the warrior wind/ of austral weather, becoming stormy/ element, strange bird/ beneath whose frozen feathers my song grew.' Neruda, 'The House', in *Canto General*, trans. Jack Schmitt (Berkeley: Berkeley University Press, 1991), 415.

24 — According to Neruda, 'It was the Spanish war that changed my poetry'; for the literary critic Hernan Loyola it was the encounter with the Spanish poets, and especially with Federico García Lorca, that caused the shift from a detached and abstract modernist style to a full engagement with sensuality.

And I kneel in your hard cathedral
Bruising my lips on an angel [25]

The mysticism of the flesh and matter bursts out as a poetic storm. Following this perspective, the house appears as a set of seductive and indefinable enveloping sensations. The house is built as a pure sensation rather than a composition or geometric organization; physical matter is organized as a light tapestry of touch and smell **[figure 19]**.[26]

Neruda's spatial practice is like a continuous backstage recreation, in which the house is endlessly rearranged in search of atmospheric sensations

25 — 'Entrance into Wood', in *Residence on Earth*, trans. Donald D. Walsh (New York, 1973), 51.

26 — 'The house ... I do not know when this was born in me. It was in the afternoon, we were on the way to those lonely places on horseback ... Don Eladio was in front; fording the Cordoba stream, which had swollen ... For the first time I felt the pang of this smell of winter at the sea, a mixture of sweet herbs and salty sand, seaweed and thistle.' Pablo Neruda, *The House in the Sand*, trans. Dennos Maloney and Clark M. Zlotchew, (Buffalo: White Pine Press, 2004), 43.

through the objects that populate it. The display of material artefacts produces infinite effects and cultural surprises that can be used to readapt spaces to various domestic fluctuations. In this sense, the recovery of 'the collector's house'[27] could enhance the understanding of Neruda's way of life.[28] In fact, Neruda's dwellings are not like museums but like systems of objects that can be organized and reorganized to accommodate relationships among inhabitants, evolving and expanding through time. The denizen thus becomes a curator, who understands his house and different atmospheres in which he lives as a continuous curatorial project. In Neruda's houses this endeavour would develop as the stage-setting tactics capable of producing various sensations through the use of shells, bottles, furniture and several collections of objects as the fundamental corpus for the production of space **[figure 20]**.

Unlike Rodríguez Arias's pre-structured space, Neruda's construction processes work more with specific, interdependent relations than with a global formal idea. The houses that Neruda designed were never a whole or pre-determined geometry but a set of pieces to be assembled and rearranged. Perhaps this logic of assembling had more to do with the Construction Principle on which Heinrich Klotz based his interpretation of architectural production after the classic modern period. According to Klotz, 'the materials that [post-classical modern architecture] uses to create a form are the individual elements of an assembled framework and not the large-scale units of the primary forms'.[29] In the hands of Neruda, architecture becomes an endless process of assembling and dissembling, the recreation of different stage settings to envelop the experience of dwelling into sensuality and material pleasure. Only as a continuous process of doing and undoing, weaving and unravelling, can Neruda's spatial practices be understood. **[figure 21]**

27 — It is the inhabitant understood as the curator of his home exhibition. Sylvia Lavin has tried to develop a complete understanding of contemporary architecture through the vision of the architect as a curator. Sylvia Lavin, 'The Temporary Contemporary', *Perspecta* 34 (2002), 128–135.

28 — One of the fathers of Chilean Modern architecture, Sergio Larrain, also gave this sense to his own house in Lo Contador, Santiago de Chile. In this house the architect placed an important collection of pre-Columbian art (that has recently been transferred to the Museum of Pre-Columbian Art of Santiago). His house appears as a negotiation between a radical modernity and a museographical use, which has a lot to do with the recognition of other cultures and a particular material sensibility. Later, Larrain's son, who had lived in the house during his childhood, would photograph Neruda's house in Isla Negra for Neruda's eponymous book of poems. See Jocelyn Froimovich, 'Sensibilidad Moderna a partir del genuino Colonial. Casa Sergio Larrain en lo Contador', Research Seminar, Pontificia Universidad Católica de Chile, 2003. (I thank Fernando Perez Oyarzun for this information.)

29 — Heinrich Klotz, 'Revision of the Modern – Vision of the Modern', in *Architectural Design* 6 (1986), 26–30.

[Figure 18] Some details of the material layers present in Neruda's houses. Stone, wood and colourful glass generate sensual atmosphere, pursuing the notion of the house as a pure material sensation.
Photo: Francisco González de Canales and Nuria Álvarez Lombardero.

An Open Conclusion

If Rodríguez Arias (and the GATCPAC) proposed an architectural system that was capable of integrating the material context in which the buildings had to be inserted, fixing the relation as stable and defined, Neruda opened up the very same relationship through a more dynamic process of continuous empirical testing and examination – the fruit of a hybrid expression of building and dwelling. Certainly, the results of this process are still tentative, but suggest an alternative to GATCPAC management of the relationship between an architectural project, and material and cultural pre-existences. Thus, they contest the relationship between the universal (objective) and the particular (subjective), present in GATCPAC's claim on the Mediterranean culture. In order to reconcile the universal and the particular, and still keep the modernist agenda alive, GATCPAC had to maintain their segregation while simultaneously synthesizing them into a single, all-embracing ideological apparatus that fixed the relationship between the two in time and space. This procedure led to the untenable collages between the universal and the vernacular in Errázuriz House, Villa Mandrot, house in Les Mathes, houses in Garraf or Germán Rodríguez Arias's initial proposals for Neruda's houses. The radical synthesis of the dialectical – of big and small orders, the subjective and the objective, the rational and the irrational – managed as an enormous single apparatus that maintains internal segregations as a fixed and unmovable image has usually been understood as the strategy of the European fascisms.[30] Consequently, it is not surprising that several scholars have found many links between the GATCPAC and the *noucentisme*, the conservative nationalist movement that appeared in Catalonia at the beginning of the twentieth century.[31]

Trying to avoid the path of the so-called reactionary modernisms, Neruda's contestation of

30 — This is Peter Sloterdijk's most influential interpretation of the socio-cultural condition of the Third Reich. See Peter Sloterdijk, Im selben Boot: Versuch über die Hyperpolitik (Frankfurt, 1993), 31–37.

31 — The *noucentisme* brings together the Catalan movements of the first decades of the twentieth century, which tried to legitimize the idea of a nation through the authenticity of its rural and natural landscape. The writer Eugeni D'Ors or the painter Joaquím Sunyer, and even the early Joan Miró, represented this very conservative, Catholic and patriarchal Catalonia. Paradoxically, the supposedly Republican, secular and liberal Catalonia of the 1930s sometimes seemed to use the same moral arguments and even the same slogans as the Catalan *noucentismo* – that is to say, a 'humanized' architecture, natural and authentic, particular to the region, lyrical, emotional and eternal. As an example of such critique see, for instance, Pizza, 'The Mediterranean: Creation and Development of a Myth', in *Josep Lluís Sert and the Mediterranean*, 14–45.

[Figure 19] The bar at Isla Negra house, c. 1956, with shells, bottles, miniatures and figureheads becoming the main corpus of the production of space. In particular the location of objects at the top of the windows regulates the relationship between the inside and outside in a dynamic and playful way. **Photo: Antonio Quintana. Pablo Neruda Foundation Archive, Santiago de Chile.**

[Figure 20] An example of Pablo Neruda's spatial practices: in this case, the production of atmospheric effects through a theatrical display of his collection of figureheads. **Photo: Luis Poirot.**

GATCPAC's *modus operendi* is a commentary on the importance of a continuous consideration of pre-existing elements as manifestations of a fluctuating and multiple reality, opening an alternative path of experimentation, also explored in other contemporary Latin American practices, such as those of Juan O'Gorman or Lina Bo Bardi.[32] In Neruda's case, the poet endlessly rebuilds his houses, and by doing so, he continually examines the material layers of his life. Through interminable trials as an empirical recognition of his tangible reality, he daily rearranges the ambiences that configure his living environment. Hence, the house clings to daily life as impure and wrecked as the life is itself, without responding to any other preconception than this certainty. Rooms are turned, flattened, deformed and displayed in a way that allows the flow that persists only through the endless modifications that the poet performs. Neruda's spatial practices, however, are as spontaneous as they are uncontrolled. The shapes grow along the territory as a drift of the poet's own desires, seduced by populism, saturated with kitschy images and isolated in the little universe that he has created for himself.

32 — I am referring, for example, to Juan O'Gorman's own house in El Pedregal, Mexico DF (1949–1967) and Lina Bo Bardi's *Casa de Vidrio* in Morumbi, São Paulo (1949–51).

Germán Rodríguez Arias and Pablo Neruda represent two different approaches to the relationship between modernist spatial production and the incorporation of material and cultural pre-existences. Rodríguez Arias set an architectural framework that could be modified by its punctual and precise contact with these pre-existences. Departing from a shared modernist project, external participants – such as Pablo Neruda – could contribute to shaping the final result, deciding on the number and quality of entities to be taken into account. However, integrating these pre-existences into the very logic of the project fixed them into a particular image of a material expression that could neither be contested nor modified through time. Simultaneously, Neruda resolved this rigidity through a dynamic process of continuous testing and interacting, but he was unable to let any outside participant into the construction of his own creation, which became a highly individualistic and irreproducible practice. As a result of the increasing self-indulgence, the production of his houses grew less interesting with the passage of time, especially once Rodríguez Arias returned to Ibiza in 1957. It is possible that it was only in their diacritical interaction, in the intertwined dialectics between the architect and the poet, that the most faithful response to the problematic presented here could be found.

The Atmospheric Expression

Ralph Erskine, The Box 1940–2 House in Drottningholm, Sweden 1963–7

Ralph Erskine working in his Box in the 1940s. The small building was not just the family residence but also the architect's office. The Box served as a lure for clients, who could observe the British architect's skill in building a decent dwelling without resources and in such extreme conditions. In spite of the hardships, Erskine seems to dress elegantly while he works, as though unperturbed by anything, with the typical British stoicism of the era.

A version of this chapter was first published in *Arquitectos* 341, (Madrid: 2005).
I would like to thank Cesar Patín, architect from Madrid living in Sweden, for his hospitality and for teaching me a new way of approaching the architecture of Ralph Erskine. I extend my gratitude to Nuria Álvarez Lombardero, José Ramón Moreno Pérez and Ricardo Sánchez Lampreave for their comments and help with the first writing of this text.

First it was desolation – nothing to hope for, nothing worth waiting for – that is, what the existentialist term *desperation* means.[1] World War II's devastation of the civilian fabric of life meant the loss of confidence in humanity, the world that modernity had planned and the future to hope for. There were also those who would find in its chastening experiences something hospitable – a tragic subsistence able to offer the last chance to regain and regroup memories, experience and imagination through a particularly extreme form of life.[2] The latter was in fact Ralph Erskine's choice. With the memory of the 1940–1 London Blitz still vivid in his mind, Erskine decided to escape from the city to a small wooden box deep in the Swedish woods. **[figure 1]** The architect thus began a form of life which allowed him being-in-the-world by retreating from the society, shutting himself away inside an unavoidable feeling of loss.[3] **[figure 2]** Erskine was not the only one to take this particular path. The urge to seek an ascetic refuge in order to exist precariously and continue working regardless of the deprivations was a common cultural sensibility after World War II. 'There is nothing in the world for which a poet should keep writing, not if he is a Jew, of course, and the language of his poems is German', wrote Paul Celan in 1948. But he also wrote, 'perhaps I am one of the last who must live out to the end the destiny of the Jewish spirit in Europe', giving thereby pertinence to his marginal writing.[4] Even though it stemmed from very different backgrounds and experiences, the acceptance of the loneliness of the 'last man' was taken by both Celan and Erskine

1 — Jean-Paul Sartre's intelligent existentialist vulgata, *Existentialism is a Humanism*, defines most of these existentialist terms. Jean-Paul Sartre, *Existentialism is a Humanism*, (New Haven: Yale University Press, 2007).
2 — Massimo Cacciari developed a genealogy of the intellectuals' attitude of embracing solitude in modern culture. Cacciari's essay ends with Paul Celan in post-WWII Europe. See Massimo Cacciari, 'Solitudine ospitale', in *Magis amicus Leopardi* (Caserta: Edizioni Saletta Dell'Uva, 2005).
3 — *Dasein*, being-in-the-world, is a fundamental term in Heidegger's *Being and Time*. I am employing here Heidegger's terms to emphasize Ralph Erskine's need to reestablish an experiential reconciliation between dwelling and territory. For a good introduction to Heidegger's thinking, and particularly this concept, I recommend Rüdiger Safranski's philosophical biography of the German philosopher Rüdiger Safranski, *Martin Heidegger: Between good and evil* (Cambridge, MA: Harvard University Press, 1999), 145–170.
4 — Quoted in Katja Garloff, *Postwar Germany, Words from Abroad: Trauma and displacement in postwar German Jewish writers* (Detroit: Kritik, 2005), 177.

THE ILLUSTRATED LONDON NEWS

SATURDAY, SEPTEMBER 14, 1940.

ONE OF GOERING'S "MILITARY OBJECTIVES."

[Figure 1] Image that appeared on the front page of *The Illustrated London News* on September 14, 1940. The London Blitz, the massive destruction of the city by the German Air Force, had begun on September 7, 1940. This unprecedented attack lasted day and night without interruption for more than eight months. Fire had consumed a large part of the city and many citizens wandered through the streets, looking for some kind of shelter. In the picture we can see two middle-class youth searching among rubble for a place to spend the night. With the massive destruction, the underground stations, for example, gave shelter to more than 150,000 people. The Blitz ended on May 11, 1941, after seemingly endless days of terror. **© Mary Evans Picture Library.**

[Figure 2] Reconstruction of Lådan (the Box) by Ralph Erskine, 1941, in Ekerö. It was built by the Swedish Museum of Architecture in 1989, in consultation with Erskine. As in the case of the original, the intention of the Box is to be submerged in the woods, half-hidden among the foliage and isolated from what up to now has been the 'world of men'. The lack of communication could become extreme during the long winters. **Photo: Francisco González de Canales.**

as a responsibility, perhaps the only one that gave sense to their own existence.[5]

In his voluntary isolation Erskine experienced first-hand utter defencelessness arising from the lack of any external security references on the part of an individual after World War II.[6] The great civil orders and the social ties that had held his previous daily existence seemed to be dissolved through the onslaught of interminable bombings and the reality of proliferating extermination camps. Without the protection of the civil fabric, any particular fear seemed to be easily transformed into an absolute transcendental anguish, into a profound sense of terror which does not correspond to any specific cause. That was the sentiment felt upon hearing a siren in London during the Blitz, a daily mass trauma extending over many months, which went far beyond the specific material and human destruction caused by the bombing that the sound was associated with. *Anguish*, fear without a specific reason, was another basic term of the existentialist vocabulary. Where the fear and anguish overlapped, emerged a profound feeling of vulnerability, which men and women were confronted with after the World War II.[7]

Divested of civil bounds, an anguished individual can rely only on his own existence, his doings, his acts.[8] It is a kind of heroic pragmatism, in which the only important fact is action. It is the action that justifies the presence in the world and it is the only thing that can be trusted. The post-war years would also see the publication of the stories of Jack Kerouac and Neal Cassidy, which did nothing but explore this ratification of action.[9]

For those who experienced extreme anguish and desolation, different attempts at cultural reorganization right after World War II were totally insufficient. Humanism, the great debate of the time, could not offer guaranties of cultural reconciliation. It would

5 — A weak existence that ended up in the Seine River on 20 April 1970 when Paul Celan committed suicide, jumping from the Mirabeau bridge.

6 — It is the return to the horror of the 'eternal silence of infinite spaces', mentioned by Blaise Pascal in his *Pensées*, around 1660. *Blaise Pascal: Thoughts, letters and minor works* (Cambridge, MA: P.F. Collier & Son, 1910), 78.

7 — Paolo Virno has remarked on this overlapping of fear (terror related to something specific) and anguish (indiscernible terror that cannot be related to any specific origin or cause). For Virno, the loss or simple perspective of the possibility of losing your employment today does not only produce a specific fear related to it but a sense of utter defencelessness which acquires a transcendental and absolute dimension. Paolo Virno, *Grammar of the Multitude* (New York: Semiotext(e), 2003), 32–3.

8 — '*Tuesday*: Nothing. Existed.' This compelling note in Antoine Ronquetin's diary defines this mood perfectly. Jean-Paul Sartre, *Nausea*, (trans.) Lloyd Alexander (New York: New Directions, 1964), 112.

9 — Jack Kerouac's famous first manuscript of his novel *On the Road* was written on a continuous roll of paper, reflecting the notion of continuous action. For the two main characters, Dean Moriarty and Sal Paradise (Jack Kerouac and Neal Cassidy in real life), action is a drift without any specific end. The only relevant issue is to take action – the more frenzied the better – in order to hide a part of

be revealed as an elitist system of transmission and ordering of knowledge, which – under the promise of maintaining the cohesion of culture – justified the upbringing and exploitation of men by men.[10] It would be useless and dissolved, like a collection of neutralized, aseptic and disperse information, that in general would be reusable only as a tourist curiosity, hobby or object of lore, but not as a root or beginning of anything.[11]

Despite this overwhelming cultural reality, most of the architects – for example Luis Barragán, Sigurd Lewerentz, José Antonio Coderch, Ignazio Gardella, Carlo Scarpa, Louis I. Kanh and Fernando Távora – would make an effort to humanize the artificial modern environment. They would be the last to notice that the bases of the stage setting of modernity had been abandoned by characters whose roles seemed to have been cast in a Samuel Beckett's play. However, others, such as Ralph Erskine, would look for the self-affirmation in the self-construction of their living spaces, turning toward the formless, de-rigidified, floating, imagined, mythical and fluid, which began to characterize the action of inhabitation at this time. A recognition of the reflexive ability of the inhabitant – as opposed to a simple occupant of the abstract, geometrical body of modern architecture – was a phenomenon that was echoed by the artists of the time, from John Cage and Fluxus to the Independent Group and Cobra.

On the other hand, World War II was not only desolation. It also brought about unprecedented optimism due to an extraordinary scientific and technological progress of the society. Thousands of scientists working together originated a war culture whose attributes were transferred to the winners. The war culture did not just mean a revolution in heavy industries, it was also characterized by great developments in the social sciences. In the United States in the 1940s Theodor Adorno and Max Horkheimer

their enormously desolating experience after War World II. Partially differing with this interpretation, an interesting architectural reading of Kerouac's book can be found in Roy Kozlovsky, 'Beat Spaces', in Beatriz Colomina, Annmarie Brennan and Jeanni Kim (eds.), *Cold War Hothouses. Inventing postwar culture from cockpit to Playboy* (New York: Princeton Architectural Press, 2004), 190–215.

10 — This is, for instance, Peter Sloterdijk's reading in his lecture *Regeln für den Menschenpark: Ein Antwortschreiben zu Heideggers Brief über den Humanismus* (Frankfurt: Suhrkamp, 1999); (transcript of a lecture given in Basel, 15 June 1997). Spanish edition: *Normas para el parque humano: Una respuesta a la carta sobre el humanismo* (Madrid: Siruela, 2000).

11 — It would be interesting to take into account Martin Heidegger's influential position at the time: a triple rejection of Christianity, Marxism and what he called 'the false humanism' (in response to Sartre's *Existentialims is a Humanism*), found in his *Letter on Humanism* (1946). Martin Heidegger, 'Letter on Humanism,' in *Basic Essays* (San Francisco: HarperCollins Publishers, 1993), 213–266.

undertook their preliminary research of the new, flowering mass culture (1941) while at the same time Claude Lèvi-Strauss was gathering the data at the New York Public Library with which he would later develop the elemental structure of parentage (1949), his inaugural work of structural anthropology. We realize by now that architecture in the second half of the twentieth century was more influenced by the impact of these new human sciences than by new building techniques.[12]

The celebrated houses for the Case Study programme promoted by John Entenza in the late 1940s and early 1950s, and represented by designs by architects such as Craig Ellwood, Pierre Koenig, Raphael Soriano, Eero Saarinen and Charles Eames, were paradigmatic examples of the socialization of the war culture. This tendency would soon be followed by similar experimental programmes in England and in the Scandinavian countries.[13] Not only was the machine seen as something positive but also as a heroic and triumphant instrument that had helped to win the war. The machine would be incorporated into daily life, giving a new impulse to the domesticity based on a new

12 — This genealogy of encounters between techno-scientific culture, the masses, spectacle and consumerism begins with Adorno and Horkheimer's *Culture Industry* (1941), followed by Paul Ricoeur's *Universal Civilization and National Cultures* (1951), Guy Debord's *The Society of Spectacle* (1968) and Jean Baudrillard's *Culture and Simulacrum* (1978). For the importance of human sciences in the formation of the experimental groups of the 1960s and 1970s, see Francisco González de Canales, 'Portrait of the Architect as a Young Man', in *First Works: Emergent Architectural Experimentation of the 1960s and 1970s* (London: AA Books, 2009), 21–27.

13 — Around the 1950s, Alison and Peter Smithson's proposal for *The House of the Future* (1956) and Reyner Banham's theorization of the Second Machine Age generated a climate of speculation on the future of domesticity in England in form of capsules, gadgets and other technological devices, exemplified by David Greene's remarkable *Living Pod* (1966). In the Nordic countries, and especially in Sweden, this speculation would take a more pragmatic and less ludic direction. From the 1940s on, Swedish industry developed sophisticated wood prefab systems with an extraordinary impact in the Nordic region. In this field the work of the Swedish architect Sven Markelius is particularly relevant. Markelius developed a prefab system of recombinable modules, preventing seriality and repetition of fast-track housing development after War World II, but without losing all the benefits of industrial mass production. This system was first put into practice in his own house in Kevinge, near Stockholm, built in 1944–5.

degree of empirical 'efficiency' developed during the war, and which would be reflected even by Erskine himself, who almost always worked with sophisticated technologies.[14] Consequently, Erskine's second house (in Drottningholm) was the beneficiary of Reyner Banham's Second Machine Age – as the assimilation of wartime technological development.[15] Banham's claims reached their climax in the United States through examples such as Jay Swayze's Subterranean House (1962) as Beatriz Colomina accurately pointed out.[16] However, incorporation of the new construction techniques is not the only face of this phenomenon. In Swayze's house all the elements of the other great transferences triggered by the war culture would also be incorporated: the mechanisms necessary for the control of the masses, something already achieved by the German National Socialism, but this time channelled through consumerism and mastery of mass media.[17] The *culture industry,* the new postwar form of production, would be responsible for making fantasies of the masses into suitable objects of consumption within the frame of the daily dimension of material existence. This conjunction between pragmatism and desire, between material value and symbolic value, had already been exposed in the United States through some incursions of Surrealism in New York. In particular, surrealist and consumable stages built by Salvador Dalí left the door open for American pop art.[18] It is the self-construction of the domestic as a synthesis between edible material and desire to fantasize, with a consequent explosion of carnal appetites, which was clearly recognizable in the houses Dalí inhabited in Portlligat or in Púbol.[19]

Hence, the activities of contemporary man would be carried out between pragmatism and fantasy, in

14 — Erskine built an igloo house with aeronautic technology: the Engström House (1955–6) in Lisön.

15 — 'We have already entered the Second Machine Age, the age of domestic electronics and synthetic chemistry, and can look back on the First, the age of power from the mains and the reduction of machines to human scale, as a period of the past.' Reyner Banham, *Theory and Design in the First Machine Age* (New York: Praeger, 1967), 10.

16 — See Beatriz Colomina, *Domesticity at War* (Barcelona: Actar, 2007), 279–283.

17 — As early as 1941 Adorno and Horkheimer remarked on the deep social transformation due to the mass media affecting all social strata. In the eyes of these Marxist critics cultural experience became more fake, simpler, banal and mystified. Majority of TV broadcasting from 1945 on would be fundamental in shaping this new socio-cultural condition. See Theodor Adorno and Max Horkheimer, 'The Culture Industry: Enlightenment as Mass Deception', in *Dialectics of Enlightenment. Philosophical Fragments* (Stanford, CA: Stanford University Press, 1941), 94–136.

18 — *The Dream of Venus,* an installation created by Salvador Dalí for 1939 New York World's Fair, stands as a perfect example of persuasive and consumer-based Surrealism in New York. First attempt at the interpretation of this work from an architectural point of view can be found in Rem Koolhaas, *Delirious New York: A Retroactive Manifesto for Manhattan* (New York: Monacelli Press, 1994), 274–6.

19 — A very interesting publication on Salvador Dalí's houses was produced in conjunction with a large exhibition

a hybrid space in which consumption mutates into being a creative configuration of personal environment. The second house that Ralph Erskine built for himself in Sweden (Drottningholm, 1963–7) puts into question the latency of his first Nordic house, The Box: How were people to live in the aftermath of the war? How were they to start living distinctly from what until then had been seen as civilized? Or, better yet, how were they to take advantage of this historical rupture to recuperate all that had been sacrificed by the previous 'civilizing' process?

on Dalí's relationships with architecture at Foundation Caixa Catalunya. Juan José Lahuerta's contribution is especially relevant, and a vital complement to his essay *El Fenómeno del Extasis*, published a few years later. Montserrat Aguer (ed.), *Dalí Architecture: from June 19 to August 25, 1996, La Pedrera* (Barcelona: Fundació Gala-Salvador Dalí and Fundació Caixa de Catalunya, 1996); Juan José Lahuerta, *El fenómeno del éxtasis. Dalí ca. 1933* (Madrid: Ediciones Siruela), 2004.

The two houses that Erskine constructed for himself are offsprings of a pioneering initiative in the understanding of 'mutual belonging' that helps us build an alternative frame for natural and human connections. Erskine's experience allows us to return to establishing a relationship with the earth and others through the logic of the sensible: the logic which tries to surpass an analyticalal/productivist approach in order to realise an architecture which roots the relations between the human and the environment through the practice of everyday life.

New Empiricism

In 1947 an article about the new Nordic architecture, particularly Swedish, appeared in an issue of the *Architectural Review*. It was entitled 'The *New Empiricism*' and accompanied by images of three houses: by Ralph Erskine, Sven Markelius and Sture Frölén. The text, signed by the editorial team (J. M. Richards, Nikolaus Pevsner, Osbert Lancaster and Hubert de Cronin Hastings),[20] justified its title by tracing a new way of making modern architecture, which consisted of a 'synthesis between rationalism and empiricism'. Their analysis would later be extended to the 'synthesis between craftsmanship and industrialization', 'technology and traditional knowledge', and finally, between 'rural and urban'. Six month later, in the same magazine, Eric de Maré wrote using similar terms – that is, recognizing in this architecture a means toward 'humanization' of

20 — 'The *New Empiricism*, Sweden's latest style,' in *Architectural Review*, 101 (June 1947), 199–204. The influence of Gordon Cullen, a friend of Erskine, is notable in this issue of the magazine.

the modern movement, or in Maré's own words, 'to recupera[tion of] domestic comfort, common sense, traditional textures and colours, fantasy and taste for decoration, the value of craftsmanship'.[21] **[figure 3]**

In August 2004 I paid a visit to Ralph Erskine at his house in Drottningholm and afterwards I went to see his Box, his first self-constructed house mentioned in the *Architectural Review*.[22] I hardly seemed to find anything of what the British magazine had expressed. Ralph Erskine appeared to me, and still does, alien to the movement that would later be compared with the miseries of Italian realism. Manfredo Tafuri accused the Swedish movement of being 'petit bourgeois and retrograde pseudo-utopias based on the recuperation of the architecture's status as craft',[23] a charge quite incongruent with Erskine and his architecture, which was always most technologically advanced. Stefano Ray, who was the first expert on Erskine, seemed more accurate. According to him, only this emigrant architect, who had come from a pragmatic culture, 'made the effort to contribute significant forms on which a continuous confrontation with the authentic demands of reality could be based'. Thus, Erskine gave sense to the word *funkis*, the moniker under which the Swedish functionalism is known, but which in its most exact translation means 'to be useful, to serve, to participate', as Stefano Ray pointed out at the beginning of his book.[24]

21 — Eric De Maré, 'The New Empiricism. Or the antecedents and origins of Sweden's latest style', in *The Architectural Review* 103 (Jan. 1948), 9–22.
22 — In reality, it is a reconstruction of the original house built under direction of Erskine for the Swedish Museum of Architecture in 1989. The original Box was constructed by Erskine in 1941–2.
23 — Manfredo Tafuri, 'Réalisme et Architecture', in *Critique* 476/477 (Jan/Feb. 1987), 23–42. Translation mine.
24 — Stefano Ray, *Ralph Erskine: architteture di bricolage e partecipazione*, (Bari: Dedalo libri, 1978), 5. Translation mine.

The Experience of The Box

Lådan, The Box, is a small house in shape of a drawer, constructed using discarded materials, which Erskine erected between 1941 and 1942. It is located half way up a moderate slope and faces a vast valley in Lissma on the outskirts of Stockholm. The interior is a single room functioning as a living room/bedroom/office and divided by an interior-exterior chimney that accommodates a small kitchen/office. The bathroom is situated in an outdoor hut and the water has to be taken from a well outside. **[figure 4]**

[Figure 3] Drawing by Ralph Erskine of the Box, published in *The Architectural Review* dedicated to the Nordic 'New Empiricism'. Although the articles that appeared in the issue insisted on a comprehensive rural/urban, technological/artistic, romantic/modern synthesis of this new architecture, Erskine's drawing seems to want to capture more existential content. A small black figure, as willowy as a Giacometti's sculpture, can be seen in the image, insignificant in the interior of the dense forest. The figure is alone in the exterior, in the tension between the formlessness of the immense, slender tree masses and a small geometric box defined with an enormous precision and detail. In the distance, on the far lower right side, the nearest human settlement is represented in an almost comical way, completely on the fringe of what is happening in the main scene.
© Arkitekturmuseet Stockholm

[Figure 4] Plan of the Box that Erskine built with his own hands with the help of his Danish associate, Aage Rosenvold. One large room that measures 6 metres by 6.3 metres is separated into two smaller areas by an interior/exterior chimney. Bathrooms, water and other services are scattered throughout the plot, outside of this room. Erskine constructed the house himself between 1941 and 1942, and later moved there with his wife and two daughters, who lived there with him until 1946. The original layout, with its meticulous stone pathways, is more pleasant than the later version, which seems more like a trench to shelter from the harsh Swedish climate.
© Arkitekturmuseet Stockholm

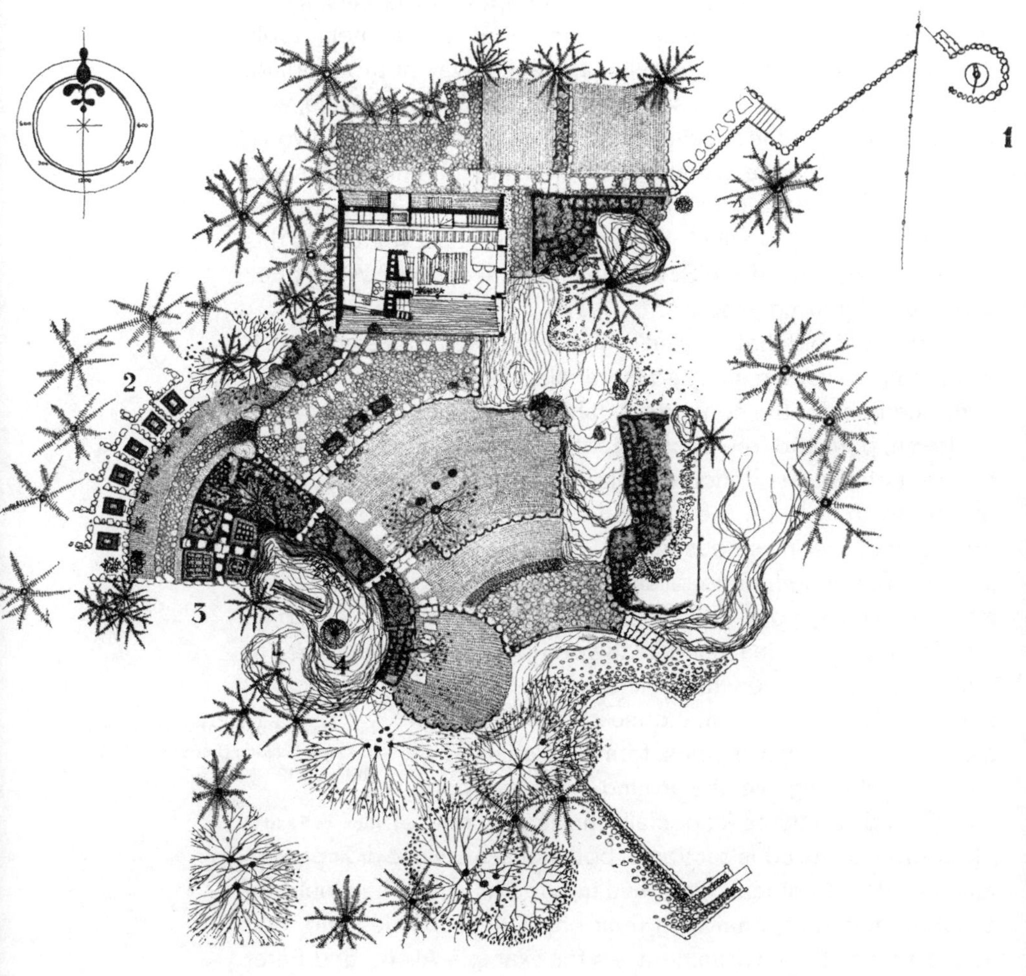
1
2
3
4

Traditional historiography of the new empiricism movement, in which Erskine's house is customarily included, is premised on the minor impact of the industry in Scandinavia, and therefore, on a more gradual transition from craftsmanship to industry and from rural to urban. This viewpoint, widely accepted nowadays, stems from a very particular presupposition – that is, that ineluctably the use of specific means implies a specific way of proceeding. However, why should we assume that was the case of Erskine, who was a foreigner to the Nordic lands? His later trajectory showed a definite interest in the prefabricated, the latest technologies and all the industrial developments that came with the War. Therefore, while approaching Erskine's house, we should ask: what does this small Box possess of the Scandinavian rural culture? What does it posses of craftsmanship?

It cannot be said that Erskine's initial approach was empirical. It is true that he used discarded materials, like an old bed-frame as reinforcement for the concrete, but his Box is still a small rationalist dream, pure and free of ornament, strictly executed according to a reductive prescription of solar orientations: more insulation on the north, less on the east and west, open to the south. In the study of Erskine's houses, Peter Collymore's definition of his work as 'romantic functionalism' neither seems to be useful. According to Collymore, Erskine's architecture 'is not subject to an outside aesthetic idea, such as the preconditions of geometry or a classic programme with which the structure has to comply'.[25] However, both his Box and house in Drottningholm are preconceived geometries, formally freestanding and subtly floating over the ground – irrefutably pre-established structures (especially the second house). **[figures 5 and 6]**

25 — Peter Collymore, *The Architecture of Ralph Erskine* (London: Academy Editions, 1994), 34.

Moreover, in the construction of both houses Erskine did not even use a kind of empirical deductive method, in which he would try different materials, analyzing their physical properties and their adaptation to the environment, as for example Alison and Peter Smithson did in the Solar Pavilion in Fonthill. He simply used what was available at hand and employed his own approach to modernism and rational architecture. His empiricism is constituted by his self-obligation to withdraw in situ the rationalist assumptions expressed a priori. We can say that the architecture of Erskine's Box is empirical not in its design but rather in abiding to the consequences of its logic. The Box is empirical because Erskine experiments with himself, learning from his rationalist errors: the results of these experiments will be reflected in his next works.

It has been rarely pointed out that Erskine's Box was in fact a failure, an experiment that did not succeed, and that if he had not given up the torture of it, it was because of the fame the Box was providing him with. However, it was precisely at the moment when he had finished the Box, that he had to start modifying it. He had to cover the great windows on the south side with thick, detached wooden panels, pave the paths between the house and the outhouse with bigger stones and construct mounds for protection from the climatic conditions: the snow and the wind. He had to dismantle and reassemble the preconceived ideas, to rethink architecture from his own experience of inhabiting it. An architect has seldom been so exposed to personal experimentation with his own preconceptions.

The meaning of settling

Actually, the architecture that Erskine respected the most was Danish, especially in the work of Arne Jacobsen. In his journey to Sweden he did not look for architecture but for a welfare society supported by a rather consolidated social democracy, which had its peak between 1932 and 1947. For Erskine the stimulating thing was an opportunity to work with a pragmatic political programme, which was focused on a specific social reality, and within which he would effectively experience – in his Box – a first truly violent clash between reality and an idea. This was a violence sought beforehand, like that suffered by Henry-David Thoreau, which would be halfway between expiation and awareness. Like Doctor Frankenstein's terrible escape to the mountains, where peace and death meet on the same path, like the dirt that annihilated 'the Woodshed' of Robert Smithson, nature also ended up eroding Erskine's Box: a reminder of the 'biological' end of any human construction.

[Figure 5] Photo of the reconstruction of the Box: a rational, geometrically well-defined box, floating imperiously above the landscape. Erskine's empiricism began later, once the Box has settled on the ground and he needed to adapt to the more specific conditions of his surroundings. **Photo: Francisco González de Canales.**

[Figure 6] Erskine's woodshed in the rear of the Box, north façade. The initial layout of the Box had clear intentions to take the climate into consideration, though they later proved to be insufficient. Thus, the south façade is completely open to capture the maximum of solar energy whereas the north is completely closed off and enhanced with logs to increase the insulation. **© Åke E:son Lindman**

Erskine's Box tried, in the end, to pluck from the old relations with nature, from its rural setting, a new support on which to establish a whole set of relations born from the uncertainties of the present. Similar idea would be later seen in his *Proposal for an Arctic City,*[26] which parts with the belief in the inexistence of an arctic vernacular. It is not that Erskine did not know the architecture of these harsh latitudes or Eskimo and Lapp cultures, but he took them into consideration only as an instructive but insufficient experience since they did not seem comfortable enough for a modern man. As a result, he decided to create an arctic vernacular *ex novo* – that is, a new architecture that connects the arctic practices of working with totally new elements.

26 — Developed in the 1950s and present at the CIAM meeting in Oterloo in 1959.

As we can see in the photographs of perfectly dressed Erskine working in his 'office', the Box was also conceived as a space for production – rooted in the purest Western modern tradition of work as the appropriation of territory. **[figure 7]** The coin of this tradition has other side: leisure; and with it, a pensive contemplation of landscape, looking but not touching – the impossibility of embracing the thing loved. It encompasses the melancholy of the distancing from nature, which is the genealogic base of the formation of the modern. It is also present in the Box's large, open windows floating over the landscape. However, in the case of the Box there is also something unexpected. Its obvious failure and the conditions that led to it made Erskine go out to 'put his hands' into the earth. It was the question of survival: putting stakes into the ground, moving stones, covering the gaps. He was forced to learn the art of living with nature. In short, only the one who inhabits can recognize what the key issues are and this is how Erskine understood the idea of participation: 'dwellers are experts on their own needs'.[27] When the construction of a house becomes a lived experience, or even an experiment, the distance between the inhabitant and habitation is dissolved. The house gains texture not because it is made of discarded materials, remainders of life itself, but because it begins to be a mould of the body, a kind of a dress that envelops those who step into it.

27 — Peter Collymore, *The Architecture of Ralph Erskine* (London: Academy Editions, 1994), 16.

Installation into reality

Architecture is the art that has most adepts because it is about real things.[28]

28 — Ralph Erskine, 'What is to be an Architect', in *63 Perspective Jubilee Edition* (Manitoba: University of Manitoba, 1963), quoted in Stefano Ray, *Ralph Erskine: architetture di bricolage e partecipazione*, 7.

Installation is the way of making whose logic of adaptation and reversibility is capable of assimilating the speed and suddenness of fast transformations characteristic of our daily life. It is its reversibility (being provisional) that allows one to settle respectfully in the contexts charged with significance, without suggesting a substitution or irreversible modification of the existing environment. The logic of installation works as a process of a progressive creative dislocation of material culture, that manipulates the signifiers and socializes leisure time through do-it-yourself in our own daily life. In Erskine's case this form of settling came as a result of the compromise with his surroundings (occupied by things of a certain disposition, men and atmosphere) made after his experience with the Box. Erskine installed, set up, but did not modify his house in Drottningholm. It was the respect for the pre-existing conditions of the site which convinced the local municipal authorities to allow its construction after seven years of struggles. **[figure 8]**

When Erskine drew a tree, a rock or any small topographical change, it was actually there. This careful registration of the site reflected his respect for nature through the respect of physical reality. According to Erskine, only such procedure, as a part of the experience lived by men, was capable of generating a support on which it would be possible to make architecture, exercising with it a profound introspection toward the genesis of architecture as a constitutive action of human environment.[29] This turn towards actuality, which would be adapted by the Team X generation, meant for Erskine the recuperation of the sensible reality. When things are built sensibly, human language reflects secondary significations associated with phenomenological sensations or

29 — See Peter Slorterdijk's analysis in *Spheres II*, especially chapter 3. Peter Sloterdijk, 'Para una ontología del espacio cerrado' (For an ontology of the enclosed space), in *Esferas II* (Madrid: Siruela, 2004), 219–282.

[Figure 7] The shell of Erskine's second house in Drottingholm. The dwelling is compressed within a diaphanous concrete box with an independent cover that creates an efficient chamber of air for thermal insulation. The apertures to the outside are small, like winks, without large openings to the landscape. They are concentrated in specific places, looking out to the garden, which the architect designed himself. **Photo: Nuria Álvarez Lombardero.**

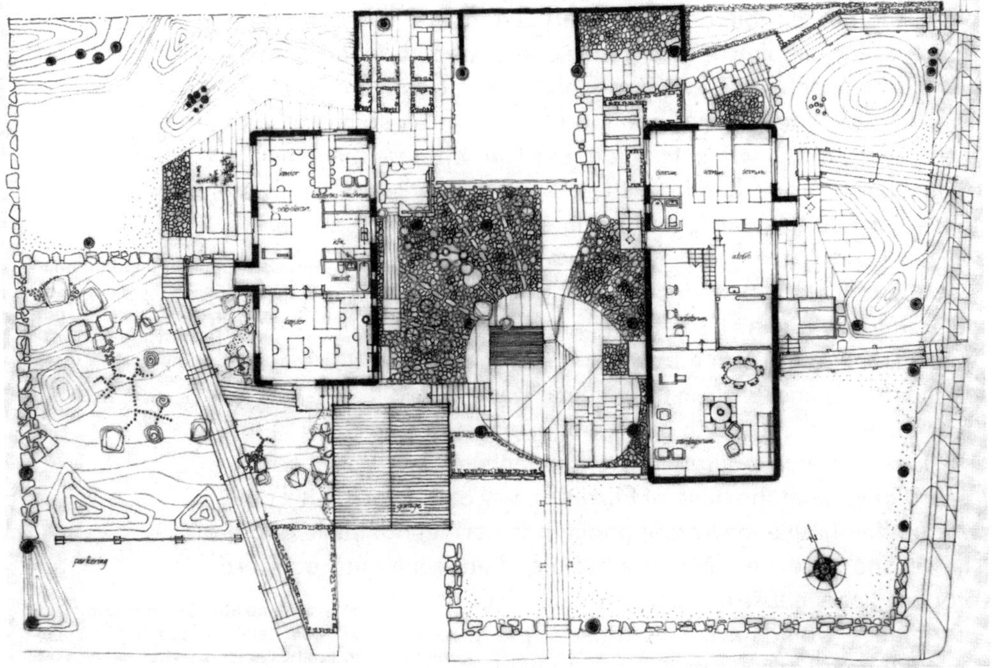

[Figure 8] Plan of Erskine's second dwelling in Drottningholm. The precision of the drawing is extreme. Each stone and tree is drawn with great detail in an attempt to reflect all of the elements that exist in reality and the exact locations each one of them occupies on the land. Unlike the Box, the workspace and the living space are in separate boxes, and a large landscaped patio stretches between them. The access from the outside is through wooden footbridges as if one was not supposed to touch the ground. **© Arkitekturmuseet Stockholm**

impressions (significations uncovered only in the poetic language). It is a more whole, complete relation with the specific, the immediate, the perceptible and with everyday things. The figure of a *bricoleur,* a champion of the science of the specific, whom Claude Lèvi-Strauss defended – as opposed to the modern engineer – in *The Savage Mind,* would be understood here as someone with the command of 'mythical language' to incorporate the sensible and material properties from the place of enunciation, in a way that allows us to establish environmental roots in the territory in which we develop.[30] This sensibility would come with a sense of instability, reflected in the character of an architect who has his office in an old boat. The Verona moved the office towards the archipelago during the summer while in the winter it was moored near the house. The myth of a mobile house, present later in the 1960s *radical architecture* with Reyner Banham as its main theoretician, would be at the base of Erskine's way of settling. In his own words, 'the house in Drottningholm has certain nostalgia about the Verona'.[31] Reyner Banham's bubble of environmental comfort proposed as a mobile domestic model – efficient and pragmatic – would have a response in the house in Dottningholm, despite the fact that the house was designed two years prior to the article 'A house is not a home' (1965), in which Banham introduced his paradigm.[32] In Erskine's case, the coexistence with the other – that is, the environment – would lead him to develop a whole series of relations, whether as climatic inventions or as forms of dialogue. They would not only surpass the idealism of control and production of the first modernists but also Banham's presupposed efficiency of the self-air-conditioned machine, which – according to a particular human solipsism – lives at the expense of energetic waste, of the exhaustion of others, something that Banham would only notice later.

30 — In order to better understand this kind of thinking, see 'The Science of the Concrete', first chapter of Claude Lévi-Strauss's *The Savage Mind* (Chicago: Chicago University Press, 1962), 1–35.

31 — Stefano Ray, *Ralph Erskine*, 78.

32 — Banham's famous bubble, illustrated by François Dallegret, was later interpreted by different radical groups in the 1960s and 1970s; for instance, David Greene's performance in 1967, as well as Ant Farm, Coop Himmelblau and Haus Rucker Co's inflatable architectures. Reyner Banham, 'A Home is not a House', in *Art in America* 53 (Apr. 1965), 109–118. See also: Reyner Banhan et al., *Design by Choice* (London: Academy Editions, 1981), 56.

Inhabiting the House in Drottningholm

The second house by Ralph Erskine is where we can find almost all the principles of his most successful domestic work, most of them learnt from the experiences suffered with the Box. In Drottningholm Erskine would bring to the level of maturity many elements mentioned before: the sense of setting, prefabrication, understanding of climate, logic of the sensible and culture of inhabiting. The house is formed by three bodies: two bigger ones that enclose a patio (as in the patio and pavilion by Alison and Peter Smithson or the Eames House) and a smaller one at the front, which is used as a storage and garage. We can find trees and some large rocks in the outside topography – only slightly modified by paths/terraces (already seen around the Box) – that were originally in the plot. To deal with the topographic unevenness, the access routes are solved through a kind of floating and zigzagging catwalks that seem not to touch the ground.

Erskine's attitude would again be to support a closed shell, a ship, a refuge, but this time it would not be open to the infinite nature – sublime and wild – but to the nature partly domesticated in the house's immediate environment. This 'domestication' consists of surrounding the house with trees, setting pieces of stone and concrete slabs, throwing floating wooden floors in the crucial places so that the topography of the site is not disturbed – as if walking on your tiptoes. A walk into nature is done voluntarily, not by an imposition. It does not have to be controlled or even contemplated. We simply know nature is there, fifty steps behind the house. It does not have to be called or evoked, because it is there, behind a thin wall of concrete, behind the trees. Nature, compared to the smallness of an individual, is infinite, and Erskine discovered the only way that a person can relate to it is through a house, and even more so, through a garden. As the poet Giacomo Leopardi wrote in his celebrated poem 'L'Infinito', the only thing that can protect a human being from the fears of the infinite is the hedge of the garden – the only thing that can calm him/her in face of the terror evoked by the flat vastness of the horizon.[33]

33 — I am referring to his famous song 'L'infinito'. Giacomo Leopardi, 'The Infinite', in *The Canti*, G. J. Nichols (trans.) (Routledge: New York, 2003), 53–4.

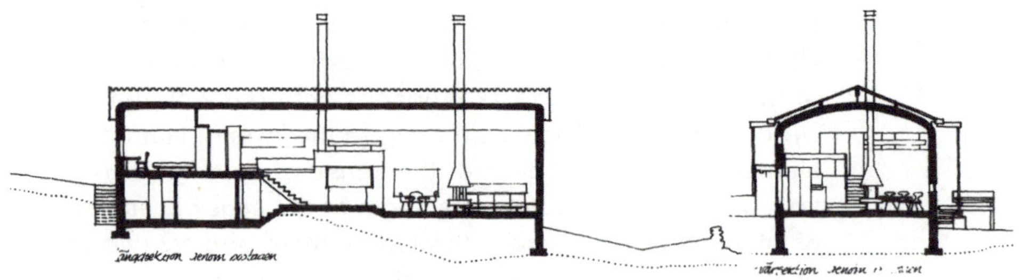

[Figure 9] Longitudinal and transversal sections of the Drottingholm house. One can see that it is actually a large, closed concrete box with the roof and some of the exterior elements separated from the main structure. **© Arkitekturmuseet Stockholm**

[Figure 10] The interior of the Drottingholm house, when I visited the architect in 2004, with the informal texture of the domestic that Ralph Erskine has given it. A multitude of objects, furnishings and other atmospheric touches completely cover the geometry of the room. **Photo:Nuria Álvarez Lombardero.**

[Figure 11] Another perspective of the interior of the Drottningholm house, showing the proliferation of small, semi-enclosed rooms, linked together by the large concrete shell. **Photo: Nuria Álvarez Lombardero.**

In the concrete shell shaping the Drottningholm house, the opening voids would not be conceived as windows for the 'contemplation of landscape' (as it happened in the Box) but they would rather be voids opened towards the interior as if they were looking into the house. Through them one can enter Erskine's tiny domestic universe, yet they are not made to look out. Only some openings on the sides give a view of the exterior patio – as opposed to open nature – and are also understood as the extension of the domestic interior. Thus, the slanted openings emerge to look from the kitchen to the garden table, or from the working area to the access to the house. Erskine is not interested anymore in controlling or dominating nature, only in his own interior.

From a climatic point of view, this prefabricated concrete shell is what Erskine learnt could be a true shelter from the extreme conditions. Apart from the formal forcefulness, Erskine designed a whole set of complementary climatic controls that help endure cold winters, making space for the new Nordic vernacular. In this house one can see a whole set of technical inventions: separation of the salient elements of the compact and closed shell of the house (to avoid thermal bridges) or the lateral poles that help the snow slide from the eaves, protecting from the fall of icicles. One of the most interesting features is the split between the roof and the concrete slab, allowing ventilation which favours a greater insulation due to the layer of snow on the roof surface. In contrast to the traditional roof with pronounced inclination, from which the snow slides off, Erskine learned from animals and indigenous cultures to use the snow as insulation. **[figure 9]**

The texture of domesticity

The concrete shell shaping the Drottningholm house is structurally a completely diaphanous body, which Erskine filled with small daily operations. Domestic nooks and low-key programmes are set within this large, controlled interiority. These domestic settings seem to be transversal in relation to the spaces they face, distorting the position an occupant takes in relation to them. They create a continuity of turns that give us the feeling of comfort as soon as we start moving through the house, performing each activity that is offered to us. For example, when we are at the dressing table, the glass niche in which it is placed seems to be a hidden bedroom window, giving the exterior a character of interiority and the other way around. The clothes rack on the way to the bedroom allows the last view through the hanging jackets of those who are in the other rooms of the house (almost an espionage tactic). Since the section of the house is a cascade, one can observe almost everything from the access to the bedroom. As this arrangement clearly manifests, Erskine is interested in controlling not the exterior but his own interior. **[figure 10]**

With the house articulated by particular installations that conduct and enable acts of inhabitation, the architect is submerged in the texture of the daily life itself. In Erskine's case the correction of the modern models is nourished by his own experiences as the inhabitant, so the house starts to become the extension of the architect's own body. From this point on, Erskine is swept away by the dreams of the inhabitant: the unintelligible relations, re-qualification of waste, accumulation of objects, memories and symbols. He collects, stores and puts away, but also suffers the worries and unease of his own dreams, desires and changes. **[figure 11]**

The house became a small perfect word, the theatre of the perfect to which Jean-Paul Sartre referred to in *Nausea*, where everything seems to fit according to the image of the world's creator, the small god of the domestic. The house ends up resembling a mirror or a projection of oneself that cannot be understood as anything other than an indirect form of the cult of the self. The inhabitant's love of boats, his raincoats, long walks, his collections of books and indigenous art: everything is enclosed in this world of perfection. The person who loves this personal world remains somewhat a narcissist, but on the other hand, it is precisely this first projection that enables him to open himself up to others, to those mute and unnamed visitors who have accompanied him through these scenes from the very first moment.

The Cast of Life

Charles and Ray Eames, The Eames House, California 1945–54

Charles and Ray Eames reflected in their house.

A version of this chapter was first published in *Summa+* 112, Buenos Aires, 2010.
I would like to thank Nuria Álvarez Lombardero, Fernado Díez, Aliki Economides, Sarah Williams Goldhagen, Adrian Gorelik, Juan José Lahuerta, Rafael Moneo, José Ramón Moreno Pérez, Victor Pérez Escolano, Hashim Sarkis, Graciela Silvestri and Eduardo Subirats for their help and comments.

Since the time of America's discovery, utopian schemes for converting it into the land of new beginnings have been a recurrent theme. This concept has been channelled through the pastoral idea of rural happiness and the even more ample concept of 'the good', thus making it fundamentally a moral question. From Robert Beverly to Thomas Jefferson, from Ralph Waldo Emerson to Frank Lloyd Wright, this moral construction of the good has always had a parallel in the spatial construction related to the ordinary life of an individual, or more precisely, to the ordinary life of a single family in the natural environment.[1] Significantly, the idea of the good related to the 'good life' in nature has been repeatedly associated with Ray and Charles Eames and also with the development of the programme that gave rise to their own house, among the Case Study Houses of John Entenza.[2]

Proposing their own house as an extendable prototype for the entire society, Ray and Charles Eames as designers burst into the domestic sphere of life in the second half of the twentieth century.[3] Strangely enough, this didn't happen to them because of their work on new and avant-garde dwellings, but instead, because of the furnishings that could be used in them. The abandonment of architecture in favour of furniture, cinema or organization of displays expressed their very personal philosophy of restructuring the conditions of habitability in an extremely modernized country around the Second World War. Unlike designers whose approaches primarily related to identity, monumentality or regionalism, the Eameses placed themselves in the

1 — Leo Marx has brilliantly traced the roots of the pastoral sentiment in America in literature. Leo Marx, *The Machine in the Garden: Technology and the pastoral ideal in America* [New York and London: Oxford University Press, 1972 (1964)].

2 — See for instance, Beatriz Colomina, 'Reflections on the Eames House', in Margaret R. Chace (ed.), *The Work of Charles and Ray Eames: A Legacy of Invention* (New York: Harry N. Abrams, 1997), 127–128.

3 — That was Entenza's idea: to replicate and improve upon the experiment with a prototype of a serial house for the Kwinset Lock Company of Anaheim, California (1951), that, however, was never built. See Donald Albretch, 'Design as a method of Action', in Margaret R. Chace (ed.), *The Work of Charles and Ray Eames: A Legacy of Invention* (New York: Harry N. Abrams, 1997), 28.

subtle and delicate role of self-experimentators. Their reflection had to do with the light, fragile and ephemeral aspects of daily life; with the connections and finite elements or entities of spatial production. It was a sensitive acknowledgment of the emotional qualities of the material world in order to enable the inhabitant to develop another kind of connection or coupling with his/her domestic environment.

Genesis of the self-experimentation project

On July 5, 1941, Charles and Ray Eames arrived in Los Angeles excited about the possibility of enjoying a better climate and obtaining work as industrial designers thanks to the industrial push taking place in the region because of the War.[4] The main war industries had positioned themselves in California, which had lead to a change in density in the country, rapidly displaced toward the West.

Los Angeles solidified its position as the aviation capital of the United States. Major aircraft companies such as Douglas, Lockheed, and Vultee employed many of those who emigrated to Los Angeles region in search of high-paying defence work. In the eyes of designers like the Eames, these companies also projected a compelling vision of the future through the industrial architecture of their new aircraft factories and advanced materials and technologies of their flying machines.[5]

Once the war was over California would retain this privileged position, leading technological development of the country, being also the region that better socially absorbed wide ranging innovations in daily life, from photographic cameras, computers, automated toys, innovative materials such as plastics, to small electronic devices and other 'charming' novelties.[6] A few years before, in 1938, John Entenza, an active young journalist

4 — It is important to remember that Ray was from California and was not at all comfortable with the weather of the Midwest. Besides, upon arriving, Charles and Ray wanted to develop in the war industry the models of laminated wood that they had already developed before leaving for California, along with Eero Saarinen, at Cranbrook. The accuracy of the date is referenced in Eames Demetrios, *An Eames Primer* (New York: Universe Pub., 2001), 100.

5 — Donald Albrecht, 'Introduction', in *The work of Charles and Ray Eames: A legacy of invention*, 114.

6 — Beatriz Colomina, 'Cold War/Hothouses', in Beatriz Colomina et al. (eds.), *Cold War Hothouses: Inventing Postwar Culture from Cockpit to Playboy* (New York: Princeton Architectural Press, 2004), 10–21.

connected with the world of culture and art, who had also recently arrived in California, decided to join *California Arts and Architecture* magazine. Five years later, in 1943, when the magazine was established and the United States was starting to envision the form of its post-war reconstruction, he sponsored a peculiar program of experimental housing. The idea was to create new domestic environments for post-war America, taking advantage of the technological advances the war produced.[7] Two years later the theoretical proposals became a real programme that transformed every produced dwelling into an experiment or a case study which tried to fulfil the cultural agenda of the North American pastoral tradition, based on the moral concept of 'good living conditions for eight American families'.[8] **[Figure 1]**

Around 1945 Entenza called upon Charles Eames and Eero Saarinen to design two houses for his Case Study House programme, since the Eameses had been part of the editorial board since 1942. One of the houses, the Case Study House #8, would be for Charles and Ray, and the other, the Case Study House #9, would be for John Entenza, both of which would be published in *Arts and Architecture* in 1945.[9] Entenza's house was built approximately as it was first published, but the Eames' house underwent a severe change from the first publication. At first the house was called the *bridge-house*, and it was a sort of cantilevered pavilion similar to the Glass House on a Hillside that Mies Van der Rohe had proposed in 1934 and that had been the seminal project for the later Farnsworth house.[10] The project that was carried out jointly by Eero Saarinen and Charles Eames, without the collaboration of Ray (who wasn't an architect but a visual artist),[11] was also very similar to Samuel Bell's unbuilt house in Cranbrook, which Saarinen had designed in 1941.[12]

7 — 'Designs for postwar living', in *California Arts and Architecture*, 60 (Aug. 1943), 23–38.

8 — John Entenza, 'Announcement. Case study house program', in *Arts and Architecture*, 62 (Jan. 1945), 37. The initial programme involved eight experimental houses. By the 1960s it would be expanded to more than 30, and it is remarkable what influence such a relatively small initiative actually had. It is also important to note Entenza's shift in role, from an editor to a developer. See Esther Mc Coy, *Case Study Houses*: 1945–1962 (Los Angeles: Hennessey & Ingalls, 1977), 99–100. The program ran from 1945 to 1966 and had two stages. The idea of application of new technologies in the first Case Study houses actually failed, and only those numbered 5, 8, 9 and 10 had a metal framework structure. As a result, for the second stage Entenza invited architects he knew were working with metal framework systems, like Raphael Soriano, Pierre Koenig or Craig Ellwood.

9 — 'Case study houses 8 and 9', in *Arts and Architecture*, 62 (Dec. 1945), 44–51.

10 — In the middle there would be his famous project of the *Resor House* (1937–1940), with its collages framing the landscape.

11 — This factor will be important in the house's change of design. Ray and Charles met at Cranbrook after Ray had studied in Manhattan with the master Hans Hofmann and was a founder-member the American Abstract Artists.

12 — Peter C. Papademetriou, 'Eames, Saarinen: A Magic Box/La scatola magica', in *Casabella*, 662/663 (Dec. 1998/Jan. 1999), 121.

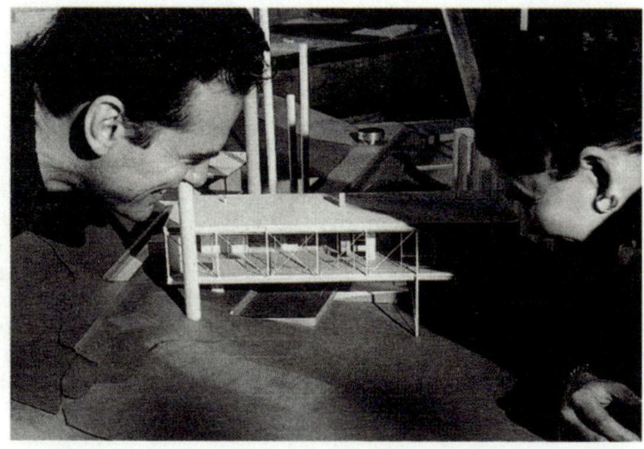

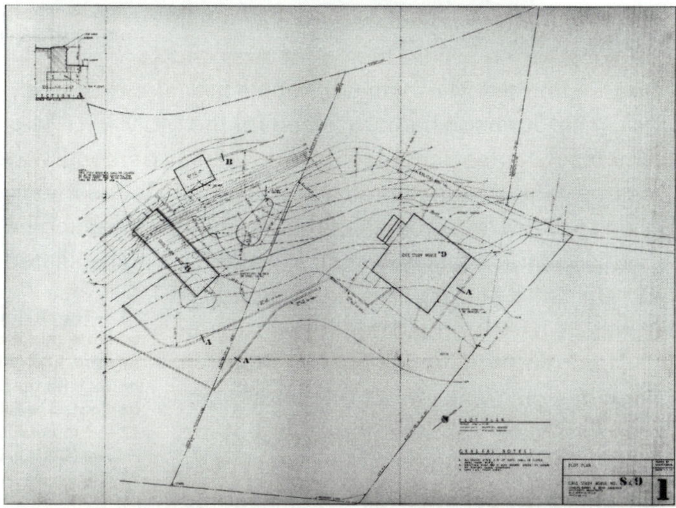

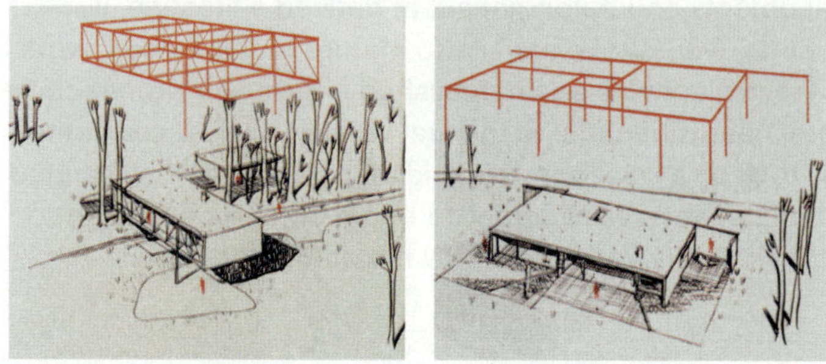

[Figure 1] First proposal for the Case Study House #8 and #9, for the Eameses and John Entenza. Above Ray and Charles Eames with the model of #8, their bridge-house. © **2011 Eames Office, LLC (www.eamesoffice.com)**

In general terms, the house could be considered a continuation of heroic modernism – of Mies, certainly – but also a wink at the palafitic architecture vernacular to Los Angeles, known as the *ding-bat houses*.[13] However, the Entenza house and the Eames House did not exactly share the same referential ground. Whereas the Eames House was similar to Mies proposals, the Entenza house could be related to Oscar Niemeyer and Burle Marx's creations, which were also frequently reproduced in the *Arts and Architecture* during those years, following the success of the *Brazil Builds* show.[14]

The seed for the abandonment of the first version of the Eames House was sown around 1947 when Charles, looking for an article theme for *Arts and Architecture*, visited the Mies van der Rohe's furniture design exhibition that Philip Johnson had organized for the MoMA.[15] It was not until then that Charles accepted in an absolutely personal way the work of the master. What Charles most admired in the Mies's exhibition was not the design of the furniture itself, something he had been working on in a totally innovative fashion using laminated wood, but rather the atmosphere he had created with it, the way he had arranged it for the ehxibition purpose.[16] According to Charles Eames, thanks to the exhibition design it was possible to understand everything about Mies's architecture.[17] At that moment Charles understood that a house was not the walls that framed it but rather an organization of personal objects and belongings that defined a lifestyle. **[figure 2]**

These ideas would take a while to mature in the Eames' work. In 1948 the project was again published in *Arts and Architecture* in the form nearly identical to the first version. Only a year later it suddenly took on a new form. It is said that the house was changed just as the Eameses were about to begin construction, right on the site itself. Thirty years later, Ray remembered:

13 — Giovanni Brino, 'Dingbat' in 'Radici dell'architectura moderna nella *California* meridional', in *Zodiac*, 11 (Mar. 1994), 48–50.

14 — See for example the project for the recreation house by Oscar Niemeyer and Roberto Burle Marx published just after the first revision of the case studies #8 and #9 in *Arts and Architecture*, 65 (Mar. 1948), 42–43.

15 — For further references see the catalogue of the exhibition: Philip Johnson, *Mies van der Rohe* (New York: The Museum of Modern Art, 1947).

16 — The chairs made of plastic fibre, which would make them even more famous, had not arrived yet and would begin with the *Chaise Longue* of 1948, dedicated to Billy Wilder.

17 — John and Marilyn Neuhart, *Eames House* (Berlin: Ernst & Sohn, 1994), 23–26.

[Figure 2] Charles and Ray Eames, publicity montage for Herman Miller, 1948. The furnishings and their volatile organization create the space.

We worked on a house called the bridge house ... It was cantilevered between these two trees. We had lived in an apartment so it would seem nice to have it raised from the ground. We liked that, and looking out to the sea. It took so long to develop and by the time we were ready to build, you know, we had come to know the property pretty well. At the last moment, it seems overnight, it was changed. Charles had said 'you know ... this is the smallest volume with the greatest amount of material. Let's see what the largest volume could be with the same amount of material.' That was like a game to him. And almost overnight it was changed from the previous house, because we'd got to love the meadow and the idea of putting a house in the middle of it seemed terrible at that moment.[18]

The house was published for the first time in its definitive design in *Arts and Architecture* in 1949, anchored to the ground and quite a bit larger in size than before.[19] This unexpected change was what Alison and Peter Smithson understood as the most genuine of the Eameses.[20]

18 — Neil Jackson, 'The style that nearly ...', in *Architectural Review*, 193:1156 (Jun. 1993), 165.
19 — 'Case study house no. 9 under construction', in *Arts and Architecture*, 66 (Jan. 1949), 31–32.
20 — Peter Smithson, 'On Reading the Black Book', in Alison Margaret and Peter Smithson, *Changing the Art of Inhabitation* (London: Artemis, 1994), 101.

Enclave and Experience

And almost overnight it was changed from the previous house, because we'd got to love the meadow.[21]

After 13 years of living in it, the building for me ceased to exist a long time ago.[22]
RAY EAMES

21 — Neil Jackson, 'The style that nearly ...', 165.
22 — Commentary by Ray Eames quoted in Esther Mc Coy, *Case Study Houses: 1945–1962*, 54.

The project's radical modification came about only when Charles and Ray began to *love the meadow.* Having made several visits to the land, having explored it, taken photos of it, inspected the surrounding area, gathered stones, branches and leaves, shrubs and snails, having first participated in the initial construction arrangements, their eye had become so accustomed to the terrain that they could not give it up. The changes in the project reflected a change of attitude caused by the maturation of the experience of the visit to Mies's exhibition. The idea that architecture could be made up of objects and an atmosphere that they could create, inspired them to go for a more spacious, higher design and thus have a greater freedom of their scenographic experimentation. The living room was to be configured like a large hangar, or rather a movie set, where they could unveil multiple stages. The bridge-house, monolithic in respect to the outside landscape as well as to the interior possibilities, was abandoned in favour of the construction of a house as an *idyll* between an inhabitant and the land, capable of adapting itself to the experience of daily life through a continual reconfiguration. [Figure 3]

Alison and Peter Smithson developed the concept of an idyll to define a specific type of relationship between an inhabitant and environment through the means of a pavilion. Their installation commented specifically on the paradigmatic cases of the Farnsworth house, the Eames House and on their own Solar Pavilion. 'Idyll', wrote Alison Smithson following a dictionary definition, 'a description of a picturesque scene or incident, especially in rustic life'.[23] According to her, an idyll would furthermore be:

a place wherein to be restored to oneself; as a source of one's energies. The pavilion is thus seen as a place made idyll; a dream of a stress-free way of life, a domain – often a greater garden – often in the pretend wild; that is, in nature.[24]

The idyll is produced through an investigation of the place, in the constant appreciation and in the adjustment of our sensibilities to the surroundings in which we choose to settle. The Eames' appreciation of a home as an idyllic and anti-heroic encounter is unique within the production of the Case Study houses since in none of the others – like those that Pierre Koenig or Craig Ellwood would build several years later – would such a sensibility be demonstrated.[25] [figures 4–5]

23 — Alison Smithson, 'Three Pavilions of the Twentieth Century: the Farnsworth, the Eames, Upper Lawn' (a lecture given in connection with the seminar 'A Fragment of an Enclave', held in Barcelona, UPC, November 1985), in *Changing the Art of Inhabitation*, 141.
24 — *Ibid.*

25 — Compare the Eames House, for example, with Craig Ellwood's hermetic Case Study House #18 or Koenig's heroic Case Study House #22, famous for its spectacular cantilevered view.

Perhaps this particular sensibility of the idyllic relationship arose due to the violence of an act that was not anticipated a priori. Sadly, the construction of the bridge-house required cutting two of the eucalyptus trees that grew in a row in front of the hill, which was an idea that especially terrorized Ray.[26] At that point the Eameses understood that their relationship with the land should be similar to that of those who love each other – that their spaces for private needs should be inscribed within the different natural and topographical characteristics of the land. As the Smithsons described it, the house would act as an *enclave* within the land.[27] The installation would be modified to reflect this sense, placing the structure between the hill and the fine line of eucalyptuses, building it into the slope and forgetting the idea of maintaining a vast, beautiful oceanic vision. According to Pat Kirkham, it is 'the change from having the house dominate the site to letting the site dictate the house's location'.[28] Especially, in the relationship that the *enclave* establishes, the artefact should first find the idyllic relationship with the land, thus acquiring a symbiotic character. In the new arrangement, the trees and the hill would effectively protect the house, in the same way that the Eameses would protect the landscape with their daily care of the surrounding flora. The terrain forms an integral part of the house, it slips into it, just like the eucalyptuses become an integral part of the construction by providing protection from the sun. Alison Smithson stressed this symbiotic conception, saying:

26 — Fred Usher, who during this time worked with the Eameses, spoke of the eucalyptuses as a notable element in the change of the design.

27 — Alison Smithson, 'Three Pavilions of the Twentieth Century: the Farnsworth, the Eames, Upper Lawn' (a lecture given in connection with the seminar 'A Fragment of an Enclave', held in Barcelona, UPC, November 1985), in *Changing the Art of Inhabitation*, 142.

28 — Pat Kirham, *Charles and Ray Eames: Designers of the twentieth century* (Cambridge, MA: MIT Press, 1995), 114.

Territory is necessary to support the pavilion as idyll, to allow the illusion of idyllic life. The pavilion in an enclave in a domain – that is important in this story – not the formal solutions which are very personal and already history.[29]

29 — Alison Smithson, 'Three Pavilions of the Twentieth…', 142.

The relationships existing within the enclave, discovered by the Eameses and recovered later by the Smithsons, thus open up the

[Figure 3] Original site of the Eames House with a hill and a row of eucalyptuses.

[Figures 4 and 5] The Eames House during construction.
© 2011 Eames Office, LLC (www.eamesoffice.com)

possibility of a new *natural contract* as Michel Serres defined it – that is, a dialogue between different cultures linked together and enveloped in the concept of an enclave in the territory.[30] Understood in this way, the enclave as a junction of folds/warps – like the object-tapestry that architect Juan Navarro Baldeweg refers to in his writings – does not exist as an entity or an object but rather disappears and is converted into a system or matrix, or a bundle of connections that cross it.[31] The enclave manifests itself as an ensemble of components and fragments that try to recapture the continuity that the appearance of architecture, by its very nature, breaks. A problem arises when we try to establish a relationship with the natural elements, the elements that neither speak nor understand our language. How do we draw the lines that connect the tapestry of the natural with the artificial? What language that we can understand do the things of the world speak? According to Serres, the Earth speaks to us in terms of ties and interactions that are manifested in the sensible world, where each member must function in symbiosis with the others in order to survive.

The experience of the Eames House opens the way to an inhabiting of the senses – the optic and haptic – that will become intertwined with the experience of arranging the constructed spaces and living in them. It is a type of experience that would be similar to the philosophical experience of pragmatism in its most profound sense – that is, returning the integrity of man to nature through his behaviour. The pragmatic philosopher John Dewey insisted, for example, on the continuum that exists between nature and experience. Rejecting the absolute objectification of the world typical of modern science, the sensibility of experience distrusts the authority of the subject and underlies the co-appearance of the subject and the object in an act of mutual constitution through a performative action. From such experience – where the human action and nature come together – emerges the modification in

30 — According to Serres a natural contract is necessary to balance humankind's social or cultural issues, organized by politics and the law, with the natural affairs of the Earth, inscribed by the laws of thermodynamics, ecology, systems theory, etc. Michel Serres's natural contract should integrate these two poles. Michel Serres, *The Natural Contract*, Elizabeth MacArthur and William Paulson (trans.), (Ann Arbor: University of Michigan Press, 1995), 65 ff.

31 — Juan Navarro Baldeweg, 'Tapiz, aire y red' (Tapestry, air and net) and 'Un objeto es una sección' (An object is a section), in *La Habitación Vacante* (Valencia: Pre-textos, 1999), 39–44.

situ of the Eames House, since on paper the project had not found the means of adapting its sensibility to the land. Therefore, Charles and Ray spent the rest of their career adjusting those means through the use of the camera, video or microscope. The Eameses experimented with themselves in this very same continuum of life, the incessant turmoil of change and constant instability. Any attempt to separate any section from this spatio-temporal flow would lead to irreparable splits, not only phenomenological but biological and vital as well: according to Dewey, the rupture of the idea of an individual or individuality can only be presented as a negation or repression of the continuum. **[figure 6]**

In the same way that a continuum exists between an experience and a situation, between experience and nature, for Dewey there is also a continuum that exists between the means and instruments a human being uses to relate to the continuum. According to Dewey, people do not simply make instruments, like a paintbrush, shovel or camera devised for a specific use, but rather the instruments also create the people. From the pragmatist perspective, the meeting or the order of things that unifies peoples and environments can no longer be defined as starting from a consensus or normative communion. The only definition permitted is a construction of a pact or tacit contract, reached during the course of the situation itself. Hence, Dewey's epistemology allows us to distinguish between a normative organization and, as an alternative, a creative organization achieved by turning to a situated experience, and brings us closer to the Eames' way of working. As John Dewey stresses:

> **The growth of the experimental as distinct from the dogmatic habit of mind is due to increased ability to utilize variations for constructive ends instead of suppressing them.[32]**

32 — John Dewey, *Experience and Nature* (New York: Dover Publications Inc., 1958), XIV.

Experience and design

The Eames' practice is not just located in the first gesture of settling on the land as an *enclave* but rather will continue through a continuous settling in everyday experience. The Eames House, and especially their two-story-high living room, is like a stage in

[Figure 6] Charles and Ray Eames' house from the exterior.
Photo: Francisco González de Canales

which the daily life of objects is infinitely organized and reorganized, according to the very flow of quotidian life. Charles and Ray's priorities, however, were centred neither on objects nor on the parameters that they formed in their space but on what was happening between them.[33] For them 'the space between two tangible volumes is nevertheless a volume', and it is in this space of the in-between where relationships are produced.[34] The facts of daily life, just as in Taoism that so influenced them, cannot be considered as accidental coincidences; rather, they are connected to the world are determine one another. Because everything is intimately interrelated, the connections are the greatest preoccupation of the design philosophy of Charles and Ray. 'The details are not the details. They make the product. The connections, the connections, the connections', Charles explained in a recording about one of his designs.[35] Thus, the Eames' work with furnishings, organization of exhibitions and continued arrangement of scenes for daily life within their own home were a constant reflection on these connections.

Aside from Dewey's notion of mingling with the natural continuum through action, the pragmatic philosophy had more profound consequences in the Eames' work, in a way that would define what Peter Smithson would call 'the new canon'.[36] Through experience the Eameses inverted the process of the Modern Movement – in which a design starts with an abstract ideal, investigation of the means of mass production and possibilities offered by new industrial materials – to take the route in the opposite direction.

There is another approach to the problem. That approach is to ignore all materials and techniques to determine as completely and clearly as possible our needs in furniture. Then to search for the materials and techniques which can most appropriately fill this need.[37]

33 — Later we will see how the same preoccupation, though taken up in a different way, is the same that appears obsessively in Frank Lloyd Wright's Usonian architecture. Wright as well as the Eameses recognized the influence of Oriental architecture in valuing inhabitation as opposed to representation, and Alison and Peter Smithson would do the same. See Alison Smithson, 'And now Dhamas are dying out in Japan', in *Architectural Design*, 36 (Sept. 1966), 447–449.

34 — Ray Eames, 'Color in architecture', in *California Arts and Architecture* (Sept. 1943), 16.

35 — Taken from a recording by Charles Eames in which he explains a storage system. Quoted in Ralph Caplan, *Connections: The Work of Charles and Ray Eames* (Los Angeles: UCLA Art Council, 1976), 15.

36 — Peter Smithson, 'Just a few chairs and a house: An essay on the Eames' aesthetic', in *Architectural Design*, 36 (Sept. 1966), 446.

37 — Ray Eames interviewed by Ruth Bowman, 7/80–8/80, quoted in Eames Demetrios, *An Eames Primer* (New York: Universe Pub., 2001), 136.

The Eameses handled the problem of production by emphasizing the perspective of a user's reception of products, concentrating on how the objects would be used once they were manufactured. They were interested in how to utilize what was already available on the market, what was already being produced and what a person did with it for his/her own use. Following this philosophy in their own home, they used industrial catalogues of existing materials:

It was the idea of using materials in a different way, materials that could be brought from a catalogue. Thus, there was a continuation of the idea of mass production, so that people would not have to build stick by stick, but with the material that comes ready-made-of-the-shelf in that sense.[38]

This change does not just stem from the point of view on the relationship between production and consumption but on the relationship between an inhabitant and inhabitation as well. The diagrams with which the Eameses accompanied the design of their home show how different activities that one can imaginably carry out in a home are the ones that have to define the house itself, with all of the plurality and versatility that experience itself demonstrates. If the space of modernity was a space of sociability, where a resident should learn to utilize the place that had been assigned to him according to a determined function, with the Eameses it is human behaviour and existing material culture that are going to determine the organization of space.[39] **[figure 7]**

The Eames' experimentation lies in the acceptance and handling of private objects and all of the paraphernalia we live with, to infinitely recreate the domestic stages we inhabit. The home as such, as it is traditionally understood, is only an artefact that envelops it all, an artefact that seems to remain on one side, dissolving into the environment that has been created by the inhabitants.[40]

38 — Ibid.

39 — We must remember that the Modern project determined that pre-Modern person would not know how to live in the new environment, and that it was the architect who would dictate his/her behavior through the deployment of the architecture that would be imposed on him/her. With this mission, for example, Le Corbusier formulated the concept of *promenade architecturale*, a method for teaching and recognizing the new imposed architecture. Le Corbusier also proposed to teach *domisme* (how to live in a house) in the ASCORAL (Assemblée de constructeurs pour une renovation architectural), the CIAM group he founded in 1942. To know more about ASCORAL activities, see Eric Paul Mumford, 'Le Corbusier and ASCORAL', in *The CIAM Discourse on Urbanism, 1928–1960* (Cambridge, MA: MIT Press, 2000), 153–8.

40 — For the Eameses a house is the disposition of the furniture and, as a result, Herman Miller's showroom is equal to the Eames' house. Both are merely stage settings for objects and furnishings that create domestic space.

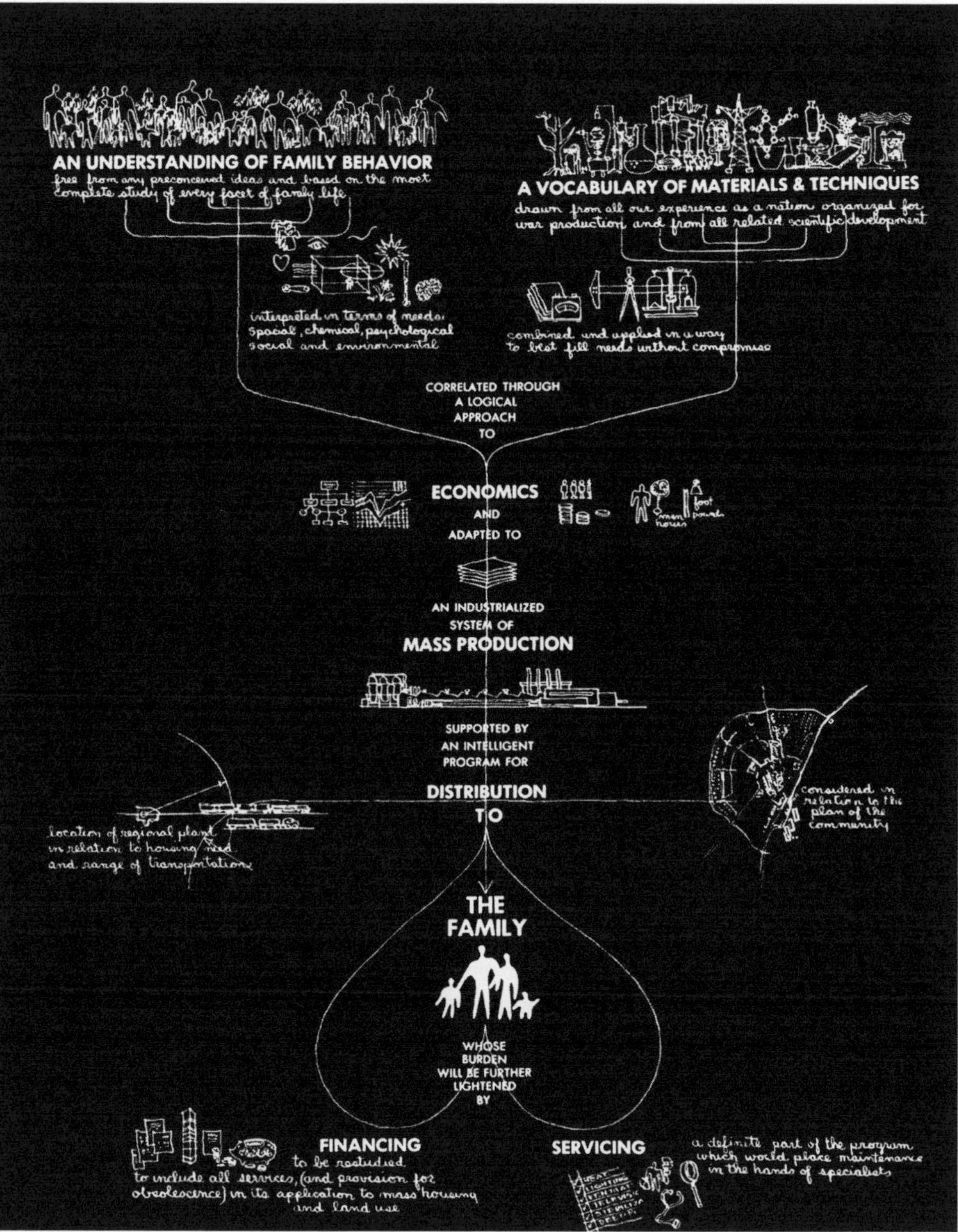

[Figure 7] Diagram of production design according to Charles Eames.

This control and versatility of the user with respect to design is what Peter Smithson identifies as central to the work of the Eameses.

Eames' chairs are the first chairs which can be put into any position in an empty room. They look as if they had alighted there – that crow in the wheelchair photograph is no coincidence, the chair belongs to the occupants not to the building. ... The Eames' chairs of the new canon are more like the pre-Courrèges clothes of the occupants; pretty, light, non-geometric, apparently casual.[41]

The Eames' dream is based on a multiplicity of self-experimental spheres of life throughout the terrain. Each of these living spheres is the construction of an interior acclimatization, like the one that Charles and Ray care for and maintain daily in their home, always unfolding new games and scenarios. From a theoretical perspective, Reyner Banham, like no one else, tried to push the limits of this type of acclimatization as a mode of architectural work, in a sharp revision of the principles of the modern masters. His extreme proposition is the well-known environmental bubble for living – a minimal membrane of a completely dematerialized enclosure, except for the necessary electrical appliances. The membrane is inflated by its own air conditioning, thereby generating its own living space. Banham's idea was to construct a true American architecture according to the pastoral dream, good life, but far from Wright's agrarian sentimentalism.[42] In the bubble the walls disappear and there is a displacement of the relationships 'between' the inhabitants in favour of an effective physical centre. What Banham's bubble shows isn't simply a hyper-techologized answer to modern inhabitation but rather a shift of the burden to the action of inhabitants. Later, in his article 'Design by Choice', Banham elaborates this perspective in greater detail. He tries to resolve the conflict between a designer and the action of an inhabitant, and explain new responsibilities of the designer after

41 — Peter Smithson, 'Just a Few Chairs and a House: An Essay on the Eames Aesthetic', 446.

42 — According to Banham: 'What is under discussion here is an extension of the Jeffersonian dream beyond the agrarian sentimentalism of Frank Lloyd Wright's "Usonian" Broadacre [City] vision – the dream of the good life in the clean countryside, power-point homesteading in a paradise of garden appliances'. And he adds: 'This dream of the "unhouse" may sound very antiarchitectural but it is so only in degree, an architecture deprived of its European roots but trying to strike new ones in an alien soil.' Reyner Banham, 'House is not a Home; Satire', in *Art in America*, 53 (Apr. 1965), 117.

[Figure 8] Interior of the Eames House: the house as a film set.
© 2011 Eames Office, LLC (www.eamesoffice.com)

the normative rules on which modern architecture was based has been dismantled:

The manner of implementing these responsibilities is not simply to assume control of the schools and expect everyone to accept architectural standards as the norm of judgement, as the theorists of the thirties supposed, but to exercise choice and background control over the choice of others, to advise, suggest and demand on the basis of knowledge.[43]

Similarly, for the Eameses design is not a question of imposing formal languages or rules but rather of creatively organizing and reorganizing by relating to the very facts with which inhabitation manifests itself to us. In 1960 Charles proposed that in design there should be no room for personal expression, but that personal expression should be shown in the use that is made of design. Echoing this thought, in an interview three decades later, he affirmed that design is nothing more than 'a method of action'.[44] **[figure 8]**

These observations are fundamental to understanding the Eameses' domestic self-experimentation as actions of inhabitation, self-expression and acclimatization of environments. Beyond the formal or material implications, the cultivation of the interior and care for the 'central totem' of the home,[45] that generates spatiality around itself, need to be understood as a fundamental contribution of the Eameses – this reading of them enabled through Reyner Banham's work. What really needs to be pointed out is that their practices did not adhere to any 'aesthetic of the machine' that Banham criticized so much in the first period of the Modern Movement.[46] If the machine appears, it is only an efficiently incorporated technique and not aesthetics. The machine recedes in order to allow life and its continuum to appear in the foreground. The liberation of life is Banham's promise and, in a certain sense,

43 — Reyner Banham, 'Design by Choice', in *Design by Choice*, Penny Sparke and Reyner Banham (eds.), (London: Academy Editions, 1981), 100.

44 — Charles Eames, 'A Prediction: Less Self-Expression for the Designers', in *Print* (Jan./Feb. 1960), 77–79 and 'Interview with Charles Eames', in *Progressive Architecture,* 71:2 (Feb. 1990), 122.

45 — As some art and cultural theorists of the 1950s made clearly apparent (I am thinking in particular of David Smith or Barthes's 'Myth Today', inspired by Levi-Strauss), by that time the core of the house had been constituted by appliances; and the appliances – the glory of modernization – must have had a kind of sacred value for the families who co-habited with them.

46 — See Reyner Banham, *Theory and Design in the First Machine Age* (New York: Praeger, 1970), 320–330.

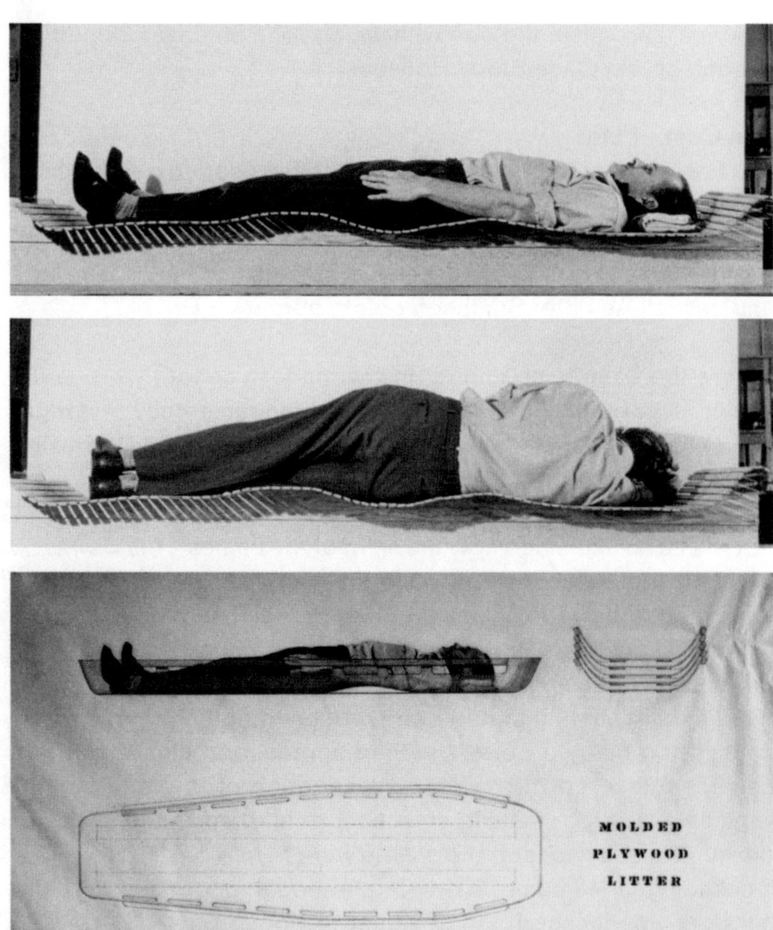

[Figure 9] Explanation of the genesis of the Eames' stretcher made of laminated wood.. **© 2011 Eames Office, LLC (www.eamesoffice.com)**

America's promise, the one with which John Entenza opened his speech on the Case Study Houses.

The Cast of Life

The Eames' designs are meant to incite the user, to seduce him/her, to make him/her feel the need to have constant contact with them. Their chairs have to be used, moved and touched. The Eames' designs are always visually attractive, smooth and curvilinear, light and casual. As Peter Smithson points out:

Before the Eames, no chairs (of the modern canon) were many coloured, or really light in weight, or not fundamentally rectangular in plan (i.e. the chairs of Rietveld, Stam, Breuer, Le Corbusier, Mies, Aalto) [47]

Sylvia Lavin explained how the spirit of the Eames' design is rooted in their first mass-produced item – wooden splints made of laminated wood, designed for the military to set broken legs – and its profound implications.[48] The secret of the splint was that it was modelled on a human leg. Rigid metal splints that had been produced until then frequently caused too many problems with gangrene, and as a result, the Eameses devoted their entire investigation of the moulding of laminated wood to making splints more attuned to the shape of the human body. In fact, the splints were based on a cast of Charles Eames's own leg. Although once his work was finished, the designer disappeared, 'the ghost of the body' would always be present in the object.[49] [figure 9]

Without a doubt, the Eames' splint could be seen as part of the infamous tradition of natural casting, in which artists poured plaster over the living bodies of their models as the basis for their works.[50] The audacity of an art that copied nature, to the point that it could reproduce it in moulds, was one of the disgraces that the twentieth-century avant-garde tried to combat. Art that tried to replicate life not only

47 — Peter Smithson, 'Just a Few Chairs', 443.
48 — Sylvia Lavin, 'Habeas Corpus', in *Architecture California*, 18:2 (Winter 1996/97), 20–25.

49 — *Ibid.*, 24.
50 — During the nineteenth century, natural casting, a practice which was still carried out in the backrooms of artists' workshops, was seen as suspicious by the public, critics and artists themselves. See: Juan José Lahuerta, 'Infamis Ars', in *Universo Gaudí* (Madrid: Museo Nacional Centro de Arte Reina Sofia, 2002), 83–89.

would have had an ephemeral consolation, but also it could exclusively replicate its own death, the dead nature, the death mask: 'Try to cast the hand of your beloved and put the plaster before you. ... you won't see other than a horrible cadaver', wrote Balzac.[51] Infamous imitative art as opposed to legitimate art (inspired by, but separate, from nature), Lysippos as opposed to Lysistratus, naturalism as opposed to the moral baseness of the practices that imitate the biological[52]– the Eameses would use both procedures without a bias, using the cast of life in their work as well as deforming it and modifing it with their genius.

Just as the splints, the Eames' chairs are shaped on the smooth curvature of the human body and not on geometric rules or preconceived compositions. In this 'other way of approaching design', the action of sitting provides the shape of a body making itself comfortable, which generates the curvilinear forms of the chairs: a convex for buttocks, curve for the back, flexion for the legs.[53] When they are unoccupied, they appear as traces or ghosts of that which is now absent.

The paradigm of this procedure is given in the Eames' own home; however, not in the house itself but rather in the daily photographic record that Ray made, testing different domestic arrangements in relation to a hypothetical body that would co-inhabit with them. As a result, the house would appear as the cast of inhabitants, of all the possible bodies that could act in it. In a way, the continuous habitation in space and the objects, presented in the Eames' film *House. After Five Years of Living,* are an indexical image of the absent body: of the Eames' own bodies that would have inhabited the space only an instant earlier. [54] Recording every moment in which they reconfigured the atmosphere of their inhabitable spaces, the Eames' photographs would be like the plaster casts of their own lives.

51 — Honoré Balzac, *Le Chef-d'OEvre inconu*, quited in Juan José Lahuerta, 'El taller de Gaudí en la Sagrada Familia', in *AV Monografías*, 95 (May/ June 2002), 10.

52 — The myth of the origins of sculpture reflects this fact in the famous story recounted by Pliny the Elder in his *Natural History*. Lysistratus, Lysippos's brother and Alexander the Great's portrait artist, was the first one who wanted to use natural casting to duplicate nature. Pliny condemned such an approach as it was supposedly robbing forms from nature rather than imitating it, producing a replica. A work of art should be inspired by the natural, but in the end, should be an effect of human genius overcoming nature.

53 — The Smithsons note, on the other hand, that the Eames' chairs began to lose their drive and return to normal in the 60s, which is why the Eames' period that most interests me are the 1940s and 1950s. See: Peter Smithson, 'Inclination of the Seat' in *Changing the Art of Inhabitation,* 103.

54 — Charles and Ray Eames, *House. After Five Years of Living* (video) in Eames Demetrios and Shelley Mills (producers), *The Films of Charles & Ray Eames* (Chatsworth, CA: Image Entertainment, 2005). The film is a sequential composition of different photographs taken by the Eameses, featuring the infinite interior arrangements tested during the first five years in the house.

The Eameses were truly conscious of this corporal presence, acting and celebrating every day as if their house had been a vaudeville theatre, urging new relationships and interpretations of their own reality. They converted their life into an unending theatrical performance, uniting stage and characters. The notion of feeling oneself a part of one's own show was profoundly taken on by them, to the point of ordering makeup and wardrobe as if they had been just another part of the set.

The Eames were very precise about their clothes, commissioning them from Dorothy Jeakins, the Oscar-winning designer who did the costumes of many films, including South Pacific, The Ten Commandments, Night of the Iguana, and the Sound of Music (Ray Eames' distinctive pinafore dresses are even a reminiscent of Julie Andrew's dresses in that film).[55]

The fissure between the absence of the 'breath of life' in the casts taken from the natural, i.e. photography,[56] and the life itself, maintained daily through the revision of casts, tried to unify itself by the means of a continuity of experience. This was the Eames' way of approaching architecture and life: finding continuity through pragmatic experience. To photograph, relocate, participate, celebrate and begin again was a cycle that the Eameses repeated to remain anchored on the side of life. Participation and celebration were as important as photography and reorganization of the pieces, which themselves fostered new performances and celebrations. The final aim was that the cast and life merge in this compulsive cycle, where the house and body are fused, in turn, with presence and phantom. 'The structure becomes so identified with its owners and in this case, owners and designers, that the stamp of those individuals becomes a permanent part of the structure itself', wrote the Neuharts about the Eames' mode of inhabiting.[57] As the constituents of the stage settings of their daily life, the Eameses also frequently photographed themselves as part of their house, reflected as presence and phantom of

55 — Beatriz Colomina, 'Reflections on the Eames House', in *The Work of Charles and Ray Eames: A legacy of invention*, 128.
56 — Remember the myth of Pygmalion.

57 — John and Marilyn Neuhart, *Eames House*, 7.

58 — I am referring to their self-portraits reflected on Christmas ornaments, the house glass facade, etc.

their bodies in day-to-day life, in which the house and the bodies finally ended up becoming one and the same thing.[58] **[See page 91]** The way of behaviour in the house was to be united with it, diffused in it, scattered throughout all of its scenarios. The Eames' philosophy of connections thus acquires its definitive moral dimension, in which a relationship of continuity and co-belonging is established between the body's performance and the settling in the material environment – something that would be replicated both photographically and ideologically by Alison and Peter Smithson, among their epigones, admirers and colleagues. **[figure 10]**

[Figure 10] Reflections on Alison and Peter Smithson's Solar Pavilion. **Smithson Family Collection, London**

The Mask House

Juan O'Gorman, House in the Pedregal de San Ángel, Mexico 1948–56

Max Cetto playing chess with Juan O'Gorman in the living room of the cave house in the 1950s. Cetto was one of O'Gorman's few contemporaries in Mexico who was positive regarding the house, and he gave it a central position in his book about modern Mexican architecture. For Cetto, the cave house develops the Dionysian and diabolical side of architecture as a compensation for the Apollonian and classical, mainly developed by the followers of Mies and the Internationalist architecture in Mexico. See Max L. Cetto, *Modern Architecture in Mexico*, (Stuttgart: Verlag Gerd Hatje, 1961). **Photo: Juan Guzmán, 1958. Manuel Tuissant Photographic Archive, Instituto de Investigaciones Estéticas, UNAM.**

I would like to thank Junta de Andalucía and Instituto de Investigaciones Estéticas at the UNAM for their institutional support. I am also grateful for the commentaries and help of my colleagues: Enrique X. de Anda, Ernesto Alva, Luis E. Carranza, Alfonso Garduño, Xavier Guzmán, Victor Jiménez, Juan José Lahuerta, José Ramón Moreno Pérez, Victor Pérez Escolano, Juan Luis Rodríguez, Ida Rodríguez Prampolini, Hashim Sarkis, Eduardo Subirats and Alejandro Von Wareber.

Necrophilia, the attraction to that which is dead, decadent, lifeless and purely mechanical, is growing in all parts of our industrial and cybernetic society ... The fascist shout of 'Long live Death!' is in danger of becoming the secret beginning of a society in which the conquest of nature by the machine will become the real meaning of progress and Man will become a mere appendage of the machine.[1]

ERICH FROMM, QUOTED BY JUAN O'GORMAN

¡Viva la Vida! (Long live Life!)

FRIDA KAHLO

Sixty years after its completion, the chimerical cave house of an architect and painter Juan O'Gorman remains to a large degree a difficult enigma to untangle. The contrast between the author's organic period – mainly represented by this house – and his Functionalist period – typified or embodied by his celebrated houses for Diego Rivera and Frida Kahlo (1931–2) [figure 1] – has puzzled critics and architects, producing an enormous controversy around his work.[2] Perhaps the comment by the influential Israel Katzman, who wrote that O'Gorman was the Mexican architect 'whose theory contradicted the most his constructed work',[3] is the one which carries the most weight when interpreting the second stage of the architect's career. Among his contemporaries, only Max Cetto seems to have shown a true appreciation for it, understanding O'Gorman's activities as the

1 — Erich Fromm, 'Los instintos y las pasiones humanas' (Human instincts and passions), quoted in Juan O'Gorman, 'Algunas consideraciones generales sobre el fenómeno del arte' (Some general considerations about the phenomenon of art), in Ida Rodríguez Pamprolini (ed.), *La palabra de Juan O'Gorman: selección de textos* (Mexico: Instituto de Investigaciones Estéticas, 1983), 50. Unless otherwise indicated, all the translations from Spanish are mine.

2 — To understand the period that O'Gorman himself defines as Functionalist, it is necessary to consult his paradigmatic text 'El arte estético y el arte útil' (Aesthetic Art and Useful Art), which in its time was widely celebrated by Diego Rivera. He himself defines his Functionalism as 'maximum efficiency with minimum effort'. For O'Gorman at that time, the only solution to the Mexican socio-economic problem was to 'replace architecture with a

development of the other, doomed art of architecture – a laudatory comment that seemed not to have had much critical impact due to the great friendship which united the two men.[4] [see page 119]

Historians and architectural critics in Mexico have carried out a considerable number of general discussions to establish the origin of the cave house, and the path that led O'Gorman to it is more or less known. Beginning with the decisive collaboration with Diego Rivera on the expansion of Frida Kahlo's Blue House (1941–2) and the Anahucalli Museum (1943–57) [figure 2, 3]; through the house for the musician Conlon Nancarrow (1947–8) to the building of the main library for the Universidad Nacional Autónoma de México (UNAM – the National Autonomous University of Mexico) (1949–52), O'Gorman's architecture of coloured stones evolves to its greatest height in his cave house in the Pedregal de San Angel. Likewise, the list of suggested precedents, including the gardens of Bomarzo and the Italian tradition of grotto, or other references mentioned explicitly by the author, like Gaudi's Parque Güell, organic architecture of Frank Lloyd Wright or the *Palais Idèal*

pure engineering of buildings'. Juan O'Gorman, *El arte artístico y el arte útil* (México: Conaculta-INBA, 2005); (lecture given at the ENAP, 9 June 1933; first published as a facsimile by its author in Mexico DF, 1934). As part of this Functionalist period, in 1932, O'Gorman founded a new School of Architecture to educate architects as engineers of construction, the *Escuela Superior de Ingeniería y Arquitectura del Instituto Politécnico Nacional*. O'Gorman developed a quite consistent practice during these years. His first Functionalist work was a house for his father in 1929. After this first commission he built another house for his brother, the celebrated Mexican historian Edmundo O'Gorman (1931), and his famous houses for the painters Diego Rivera and Frida Kahlo in San Angel (1931–2). Between 1932–4 he worked as head of the Building Department for the State Public Education Secretariat, building 28 schools with an extremely low budget. In 1937 Esther Born edited a special issue on Mexican architecture for *Architecture Forum*, where O'Gorman appears as the central figure. Esther Born, *The New Architecture in Mexico* (New York: The Architectural Record, W. Morrow & Company, 1937).

3 — Israel Katzman, *Arquitectura Contemporánea Mexicana. Precedentes y desarrollo* (Mexico DF: Instituto Nacional de Antropología e Historia, SEP, 1963), 153.

4 — Cetto places O'Gorman in a central position in his introduction to modern Mexican architecture, in which the classic discussion between the Apollonian and Dionysian sides of art is stipulated. Max L. Cetto, *Modern Architecture in Mexico* (Stuttgart: Verlag Gerd Hatje, 1961), 21–30.

of Ferdinand Cheval, have been praised in the most significant articles and books that deal with this anti-canonical work.[5] However, beyond the enumeration of this list of possible precedents, the cave house repeatedly appears to be a mysterious identity, classified as a fantastic house, rash rarity or personal extravaganza, closed to any further investigation that might look deeper into its significance or relevance. In spite of the fact that the influential *Life* magazine dedicated an entire feature to it at the end of the 1950s, raising the interest of great US artists and architects, including Frank Lloyd Wright, Mexico's architecture critics still do not seem to have reconciled themselves with this singular work of one of the greatest Mexican artists of the twentieth century.[6] Only Diego Rivera, who applauded both experiments (the case study house that he built for him and Frida Kahlo in 1932 and the cave house in the Pedregal de San Ángel), appeared to insinuate a continuity and coherence between the two works.[7] According

5 — Victor Jiménez's work is the most complete and penetrating of all these and can be used as a collection of this body of references. Víctor Jiménez, 'O'Gorman arquitecto. Segundo tiempo: las piedras de colores', in *Juan O'Gorman: vida y obra* (México: Universidad Nacional Autónoma de México, Facultad de Arquitectura, 2004), 53–73. Jiménez also published a version of this essay in Victor Jiménez, 'La casa de Juan O'Gorman', in *Juan O'Gorman, principio y fin del camino* (Consejo Nacional para la Cultura y las Artes, Dirección General de Publicaciones, 1997), 24–31.

6 — 'Mosaic – Mad Grotto near Mexico City', in *Life*, New York, January 19, 1959. According to Alejandro Von Wereber, the architect's nephew, the house had become a cult venue for several North American architects and artists, who came in groups to the open door workshops that O'Gorman gave on Sundays. On the other hand, the relationship between O'Gorman's organic work and the North American criticism began with the publication of the architect's note in *Arts and Architecture* in 1950 and the publication of a part of the house in the article 'Jardines del Pedregal de San Ángel', in *Arts and Architecture*, 68 (Aug. 1951), 46; 'Mosaic details from a house', in *Arts and Architecture*, 72 (Mar. 1955), 12–13, 30–31; 'Mosaics', in *Arts and Architecture*, 76 (Feb. 1959), 12. Subsequently, there are new publications on O'Gorman's works of this second period: Esther McCoy, *Juan O'Gorman* (Los Angeles: San Fernando Valley State College, Toyo Press, 1964) (a catalogue of an exhibition held between 12 February and 3 April 1964). McCoy also denounced the destruction of the house by Helen Escobedo and wrote an obituary for O'Gorman in *Progressive Architecture*. 'O'Gorman Cave House Disappears', in *Progressive Architecture*, 51 (Mar. 1970), 40; 'Obituary: Juan O'Gorman, 1905–1982', in *Progressive Architecture* (Mar 1982), 27. Recent scholarly work in the United States has tried to unify both periods of the author. See, for instance, Edward Burian's chapter on O'Gorman in his study on modern Mexican Architecture: Edward R. Burian, 'The Architecture of Juan O'Gorman. Dichotomy and Drift', in Edward R. Burian (ed.), *Modernity and the Architecture of Mexico* (Austin, TX: University of Texas Press, 1997), 127–149.

[Figure 1] Houses for Diego Rivera and Frida Kahlo that Juan O'Gorman built between 1931 and 1932, following the Functionalist principle the architect referenced during those years. Some authors have highlighted their anthropomorphic character as if each building were a large disguise representing each of the artists: Diego on the left, large and corpulent, and Frida on the right, under his shoulder. **Photo: Adrián Mallol.**

to Rivera's hypothesis, Mexico's post-revolutionary architecture needed a different critical and expressive position than Mexican revolutionary architecture. It is this second critical position of O'Gorman in post-revolutionary Mexico that I will be addressing: O'Gorman's desperate attempt to once again intertwine architecture and life in a densely woven, climbing floral and stone mosaic; his last effort to close the deep wound between life and construction through a sustained domestic experimentation – and so, through an exposed, naked form – that nearly ended his life.[8]

1948–56: The Scientist as a guinea pig

The majority of mortals perhaps think of their house as a castle, but the architect frequently considers his to be a laboratory. To test his ideas about housing, he and his family are capable of eating in semi-caves, sitting on pedestal chairs, sleeping in subterranean bedrooms and cultivating mural gardens.[9]
JUAN O'GORMAN

In 1947 Juan O'Gorman bought a piece of land at the end of the Pedregal de San Ángel, also known as Pedregal del Xitle, to build a house with his wife, Helen Fowler O'Gorman. The Pedregal is an ecosystem of great mineral and biological wealth, formed by the lava spill from the volcano Xitle approximately seven thousand years ago. Under its rocky volcanic bed the vestiges of the first known Mexican civilization are hidden: archaeological remains of Cuicuilco and the pyramids located in the Olympic Village in the most southern zone. For centuries the Pedregal de San Ángel was seen as a rugged, inaccessible place, befitting explorers, and the home of delinquents, beasts and vermin.

7 — Rivera, who had promoted O'Gorman's Functionalist period by entrusting him with the building of his own home, denounced the bourgeois tendency of the Functionalist production of Post-Revolutionary Mexico, and proposed as an alternative the 'American classic', the eclectic reconstruction of the native peoples of America. For more about the bourgeois tendencies of the Functionalist architecture see the articles: Diego Rivera, 'Arquitectura y demás' (Architecture and so on), in *Espacios* (1948) and 'Un pintor opina' (A painter expresses his opinion), in *Guía de la Arquitectura Mexicana Contemporánea* (Mexico DF: Espacio, Oct. 1952). Regarding his description of an alternative modern architecture in America (his so-called American Classic), see Diego Rivera, 'La huella de la historia y la geografía en la arquitectura mexicana' (The imprint of history and the geography of Mexican architecture), in Rafael Lopez Rangel, *Diego Rivera y la arquitectura mexicana* (Mexico DF: SEP, Dirección General de Publicaciones y Medios, 1986), 96–116.

8 — Following irreconcilable marital problems, abandonment of his cave house, growing isolation and rejection of the society, O'Gorman ended his life in 1982.

9 — 'La mayoría de los mortales quizá tengan una casa por castillo, pero el arquitecto a menudo considera la suya como un laboratorio. Para poner a prueba sus ideas sobre la vivienda, él y su familia son capaces de comer en semicuevas, usar sillas de pedestal, dormir en recámaras subterráneas y cultivar jardines murales.' 'Ideas. Juan O'Gorman construye su casa', in *El Universal*, Mexico, January 9, 1952, 6; quoted in Ida Rodríguez Prampolini, 'El creador, El pensador, El hombre', in Maurizio Lopez Valdés (ed.), *O'Gorman* (Mexico DF: Grupo Financiero Bital, 1999), 39.

[Figure 2] Anahucalli Museum, built by Diego Rivera in collaboration with Juan O'Gorman between 1943 and 1957, and finished by O'Gorman after Rivera's death, in 1965. After the interest that pre-Hispanic art had produced in several modern avant-gardes, and especially in Surrealism of Wolfgang Paleen, in his effort to bring together 59,400 pieces for a museum for the people of Mexico, Rivera intended to go beyond the notion of primitive art. The project was meant to be not only a pre-Hispanic museum but rather a city of the arts, with a theatre, a research centre and Rivera's workshop, which upon his death would be transferred to the Mexican national government. Anahucalli is Rivera's deliberate protest against mercantilist Internationalism that was taking over Mexico in the 1940s, and that was also reflected in Rivera's verbal polemic against Mexican epigones of Le Corbusier in the magazine *Espacios* (Spaces). The building demonstrates Rivera's concept of an 'American classic,' so much reviled by the majority of architects because of its kitschy character, but at one time standing as the memory and the eclectic construction of the American people. In the lower part of the framework we see for the first time the deployment of a mosaic with coloured stones that O'Gorman later used in the house for Colon Nancarrow, the UNAM library and in his own cave house. O'Gorman's first explanations about the origins of this cave house make reference to this American classic – and not to Wright's organicism – even though he would later reject that notion.

According to different legends it was the place of exile for those condemned during the era of the Aztecs, who were sent there to die by being bitten by the abundant rattlesnakes.

Before the transformation that Luis Barragán would make in the 1940s and the settlement of the UNAM campus, which would shape in broad outline the district's current appearance, the disturbing landscape of the area had caught attention of many famous travellers and explorers, like Alexander von Humboldt or Don Andrés Manuel del Río, who visited and described it at the end of the nineteenth century. Outstanding Mexican painters, like José María Velasco, or before him, José Clemente Orozco, would also dedicate some of their works to the area, thus extending its mythological legacy. Orozco's painting *Paisaje Metafísico* (*Metaphysical Landscape*), completed in 1948 **[figure 4]**, provides us with an idea of the landscape that O'Gorman as well as Barragán and Cetto found. It was at the same time that Barragán and Cetto were planning the first pilot dwellings for their new development of the Pedregal, around 1948, that O'Gorman began to work on his experimental house. There is little concrete information about the exact planning process for the cave house. O'Gorman appears to say that he planned the house in 1948 and subsequently built it – "with his own hands" – starting the following year, and that a large part of the project was a result of improvisation. The O'Gormans moved into the house permanently around 1950–1, while it was still being built. The simultaneous process of building and living lasted at least some 5 years (and, with a lesser intensity, a few years more), during which the inhabitants, builders, nature and dwelling were mutually engaged.[10] **[figure 5]**

The house originates with a discovery of a natural cave inside a rocky formation around which the main living room is organized as a domestic heart. A

10 — Juan O'Gorman describes this process in two different texts. Juan O'Gorman, 'Casa habitación en el Pedregal...'; O'Gorman, 'A propósito de conservación...', in *Arquitectura México*, 112 (Mexico DF: 1976), 93. (Reprinted as O'Gorman, 'A propósito de conservación...: un ensayo de arquitectura orgánica', in *Archivos de arquitectura antillana: AAA*, 11 (Jan. 2001), 165–166.

[Figure 3] Addition to Frida Kahlo's Blue House in Coyoacán (1941–2), the first collaboration between Diego Rivera and Juan O'Gorman. Conceived almost as a house museum from the very beginning, there were accumulations of votive offerings, Judas and giant papier-maché skulls, pre-Hispanic idols, as well as small format works by Frida and Diego. Juan O'Gorman had formally retired from architecture in 1937. The collaboration between the two artists would be a fundamental impetus for O'Gorman's return to architecture and his use of the popular and pre-Hispanic cultures as a critique of post-revolutionary Mexico. **Photo: Francisco González de Canales.**

[Figure 4, page 126] José Clemente Orozco, *Paisaje Metafísico* (*Metaphysical Landscape*), 1948. In this painting Orozco captures a mysterious and sublime character traditionally attributed to El Pedregal de San Ángel. In order to create this effect, Orozco seems to have melded the real landscape, the one that the O'Gormans found upon their arrival, with the refined abstraction of Mark Rothko's paintings.

two-storey service nucleus with a kitchen, office and bathroom is added to this central room on the lower floor, and two bedrooms and a bathroom on the upper floor. The two floors are connected by a spiral staircase formed by concrete ledges built directly into the stone wall. The staircase leads to an upper terrace with a glass door that permits the entrance of diffused light, filtering down through the cantilevered steps. **[figure 6]** The structure of the horizontal concrete ledges and stone load-bearing walls is covered *in situ* with mosaics made from natural coloured stones in a range of twelve tones. O'Gorman himself had gathered them from different areas of Mexico and embedded them one by one in the rock or concrete. The mosaics' iconography takes motifs from different cultures and historical moments that are freely intermingled. One of the repeated motifs is that of the *Guerras Floridas* (The Flowery Wars), also known as Xochiyáoyotl: ritualistic battles of the pre-Hispanic Mesoamerican societies in which the eagle and jaguar warriors would fight, also symbolising interior strife and the search for perfection in overcoming duality of the material world. Eagle and jaguar warriors are frequently presided over by Cuauhtémoc, normally represented as an inverted eagle, symbol of the fall of the Mexican civilization, but whom O'Gorman intentionally portrays with the head up. Quetzalcoatl, the plumed serpent, also appears a couple of times, as do the gods, the Sun and the Moon, as well as representations of Aztec heroes. Mixed among these motifs one perceives mythological animals, eyes, mouths, patterns and graphic symbols, and also elements from the Mexican folklore, like masks or the two big Judases – like the papier-maché giants from the Mexican Holy Week –who guard the main door of the house in the form of a Mayan arch. From the terrace two paths paved with large volcanic stones lead to Juan's study, on the one side, and to Helen's study, on the other. His is a unique space made up of a parabolic concrete shell covered with mosaic. Hers is completely hidden amid the vegetation and is like a stone box with a large Mayan arch finished off with rock pinnacles. Finally, the entire plot of land has been attended to with respect to its plant life, with the stone and mosaic harmoni-

[Figure 5] Frida Kahlo visiting Juan O'Gorman and Helen Fowler during the construction of the house, at the end of the 1940s. All of the mosaics of coloured stones that would later cover the house were laid by hand by O'Gorman, just as it had happened previously with the extensive mural that covers the central library of the National Autonomous University of Mexico.

ously adorning existing flora. It was not O'Gorman but rather Fowler who had closely studied the flowers of Mexico and who took charge of this meticulous work while he devoted himself to construction duties.[11] Yet, the works of O'Gorman and Fowler blend well, and the synergy between the plant life, rock and constructed mosaic also inserts itself into the interior of the house **[figure 7]**. Thus, on the walls of the cave house's living room, an impressive collection of natural orchids flourishes, surrounded by mosaics of astonishing animals, giant butterflies, jaguars, monkeys, squirrels and strange amphibians, all lit by the tenuous light coming through a pointed skylight. **[figure 8]**

11 — Helen published a well-known book on the flowers of Mexico that she herself illustrated with exquisite watercolours. Helen Fowler O'Gorman, *Mexican Flowering Trees and Plants* (México: Ammex Associados, 1961).

In July 1969 the house was sold to the sculptress Helen Escobedo, who in 1970 had the mosaics filled with mortar and painted white to address humidity issues. She also modified the upper part of the house with the help of the architect Carlo Lambrosetti and enlarged the bedroom. Recently I went to the original location of the house at San Jerónimo 162, hoping that the owner would let me look around. I recognized the enormous dwelling thanks to the fact that the mosaic on the façade of the estate was preserved in its entirety. The door was open and an impressive hubbub of people was going in and out. I then discovered that the house had been leased to the Berklee School of Music nearly eleven years earlier, and that the house continues there, and so does – in large part – the garden designed by Helen Fowler, which can be discerned among different modifications and two Ibiza-style houses that Escobedo subsequently built. In what was the original living room – today filled with mortar and a staircase with a wooden balustrade – classes in general music theory are taught, and in the upper part, where the bedrooms used to be, there are smaller rehearsal rooms. The atmosphere is festive. There are hardly any remains of the walls, though their remnants can be seen in certain particular points. Only in the garden, among back-packs and guitar cases, one can still read the letters, made of coloured stones in the ground, that say: 'To Ferdinand Cheval God's forgotten genius'.[12] **[figure 9]**

12 — Originally in Spanish: 'A Ferdinand Cheval. Genio Olvidado de Dios'

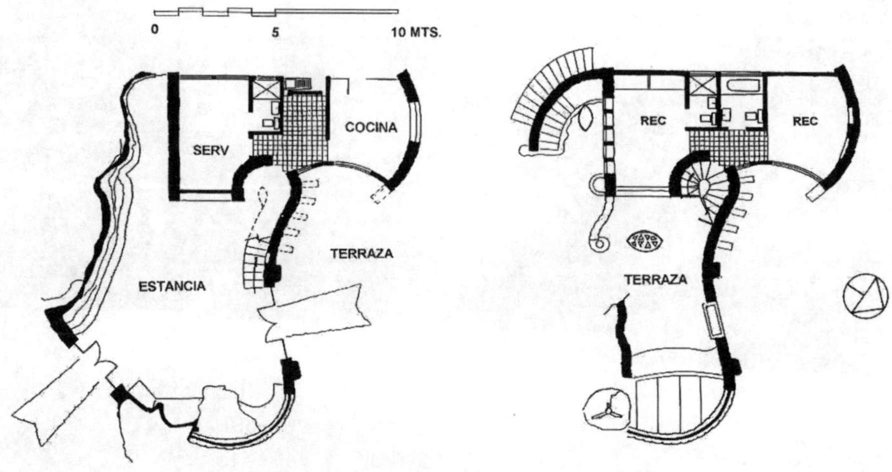

[Figure 6] Lower and first floor of Juan O'Gorman's cave house, built in the Pedregal de San Ángel between 1948 and 1956. As it can be seen, the house is organized around a natural cave on a plot of land the couple acquired in 1947.

[Figure 7] Overall view in which we can observe Helen Fowler's landscape design, colourfully intermingling with the rocky topography and with Juan O'Gorman's mosaics made of coloured stones. Flanking the entrance in the form of an arch, there are giant Judases inspired by the folk figures made of papier maché, typical of the Mexican Holy Week. Over the door itself is Cuauhtémoc in an upright position, celebrating the rebirth of the Mexican civilization and flanked by the Eagle and Jaguar warriors of the pre-Hispanic Flowery Wars. **Photo: Juan Guzmán, 1958. Manuel Tuissant Photographic Archive, Instituto de Investigaciones Estéticas, UNAM.**

[Figure 8] The spectacular living room of the cave house like a sensuous explosion of colours and fragrances. A pointed skylight spills light over a zoological constellation, which intermingles with the orchid collection that Helen Fowler planted in the naturally deposited silt among the cavities of the rocks. **Photo: Juan Guzmán, 1958. Manuel Tuissant Photographic Archive, Instituto de Investigaciones Estéticas, UNAM.**

[Figure 9] Fragment of the gardens designed by Helen Fowler in the area surrounding the house as they appear today. In the mosaic on the ground one can still read O'Gorman's dedication: 'To Ferdinand Cheval, God's Forgotten Genius'. **Photo: Francisco González de Canales.**

The House as Mask

Truly I walk along I hear the rocks as if were replying to the sweet songs of the flowers [13]

NINOYOLNONOTZA

O'Gorman's cave house is a protest against the uncontrolled development of post-revolutionary Mexico. The same criticism is expressed in his painting *La Ciudad de México* (*Mexico City*) (1947–9) [figure 10], painted in the same years he began the work on his house, and it parallels the criticism that Luis Buñuel developed in his bloody film *Los Olvidados* (*The Forgotten*) (1950) [figure 11].[14] To articulate his position, O'Gorman alludes to pre-Hispanic Mexico as a point of reference to living in harmony with the land. In spite of the acerbic criticism with which the work was received in Mexico, Juan O'Gorman's house contributes to an idea that obsessed some of the other Mexican architects of his time: the notion of the house as the uterus of Mother Earth, the large maternal womb of an indigenous woman, who protects us in her interior. This conception is also reflected in Carlos Lazo's house in El Rincón del Bosque and even in the irregular form of one of the wings of Max Cetto's house in the Pedregal, both of which were constructed during the same time as O'Gorman's.[15] Actually, Juan O'Gorman's house takes advantage of an inside hole formed by the lava, as if it indeed were a maternal womb of humid stone in which the main room of the house were to be constructed. His shelter was not exactly built, but rather it was discovered. The link between the O'Gormans and their house is born: in Juan's careful examination of the land and in Helen's promenades across the site; in the identification of a mineral, plant and animal reality that co-habitates with them. It is a question of gradually becoming more familiar with a place that has been discovered, and going about finding

13 — 'Ninoyolnonotza', in Daniel G. Brinton, *Ancient Náhuatl Poetry: Containing the Náhuatl Text of XXVII Ancient Mexican Poems* (Fairford: Echo Library, 2006), 27. (First published in Philadelphia: D. G. Brinton, 1887.)

14 — Luis Buñuel, *Los Olvidados*, México DF, 1950 (film). The film is about a group of destitute children on the edge of a city in continual growth. Each lack of understanding has a parallel with the background: a tenement building to be built, a tower to be constructed...

15 — These references were highlighted by Louise Noelle in her book about the modern Mexican architecture. Louise Noelle, 'O'Gorman, Juan', in *Arquitectos Contemporáneos de México* (México: Ed. Trillas, 1989), 108–112. Both were also published in *Arquitectura México*: Carlos Lazo, 'Pequeña residencia', in *Arquitectura México*, 25 (México DF, 1948), 279–285; Max Cetto, 'Casa en El Pedregal', in *Arquitectura México*, 53 (México DF, 1956), 41–43.

[Figure 10] Juan O'Gorman, *La ciudad de México* (*Mexico City*), 1947–9. In the fore-ground of the painting anonymous hands are holding a city map. It is the *Plano de Upssala*, the map of the ancient city of Tenochtitlán, which, according to the legend, was painted by native Indians in the Colegio Imperial de Santa Cruz de Tlatetolco. Behind the map, to the left, there is a figure of a *mestizo* worker, surrounded by tools and carrying a modern map. The worker, elevated above the city, is putting up a brick enclosure on a concrete frame on his left while on his right side he is finishing a stone wall, resembling the traditional ones used by the Aztecs. O'Gorman's own proposal is situated between the brick and the rough stone, between the future and the past, representing the retro-activation of marginalized Mexican memories as a catalyst of the future development of the city.

[Figure 11] The movie *Los Olvidados* (*The Forgotten*) by Luis Buñuel (1950) was proclaimed a World Heritage Work by the UNESCO and portrays post-revolutionary Mexico in a total developmental frenzy. In the shadow of the glorious growth of Mexico City were the forgotten ones, shedding light on an unequal process of modernization, leading to an uncontrollable and increasing violence. **© Cordon Press.**

your own place and the way to settle into it. Once the enclave has been found by the inhabitant, the cave needs to be protected and secured. Therefore, O'Gorman used a mask – just as the shaman uses it to protect his people. Octavio Paz has spoken about the mask as the main reflection of the Mexican character: 'his face is a mask and so is his smile'.[16] Yet, for Paz the mask is an image of what is closed, what is reserved. The important thing for a Mexican is to not back down, or not to open oneself up, and a proof that are traditional associations the Mexican makes with masculinity, in contrast with femininity which opens itself up to the macho. Accordingly Paz writes:

16 — Octavio Paz, 'Mexican Masks', in *The Labyrinth of Solitude and Other Writings* (New York: Grove Press, 1985), 29.

Hermeticism is one of the several recourses of our suspicion and distrust. It shows that we instinctively regard the world around us as to be dangerous. ... The harshness and hostility of our environment and the hidden, indefinable threat that is always afloat in the air, oblige us to close ourselves in, like those plants that survive by storing up liquid within their spiny exterior.[17]

Paz's thoughts reflect the persistence of the traditionalist Hispanicism – the bleakest legacy of the colonial Spain, with its superfluous nobility and perverse compassion, in post-revolutionary Mexico. That Spain that was intransigent and self-righteous, suspicious, chaste, virile and full of self-imposed pain. 'We are taught from children to accept suffering with dignity', Paz claims:[18] a tradition that hides and blames life, and leads to a penitent seclusion. This is the mask of solitude, the mask that preserves its own guilt, which is different from the mask that O'Gorman offers, the shaman's mask: the one that does not close off or silence but rather serves to communicate with other worlds.

17 — Octavio Paz, 'Mexican Masks', 30.
18 — Octavio Paz, 'Mexican Masks', 31.

Architecture as a mask has also been deeply studied by the New York architect John Hejduk, who since the early 1980s began to install habitable figures of a carnavalesque nature in different cities of the world. **[figure 12]** Hejduk's masks are at one and the same time the occlusion and the expression of dwelling, and perhaps their origins lie in certain minimalist artistic practices common in New York of the 1960s. For example, in a piece by Sol Lewitt of that era, the artist erased those parts of a photographic plan of cities where he had lived or that he was acquainted with.[19] For Hejduk the house starts with this same issue of covering the lodging, of denying it, in order to give it freedom and expression. In a kind of Adornian negative dialectics, the poetic instrument of solipsism attempts to revive the formless poetics of life that the glass box of American corporate architecture has negated.[20] Although this is also the argument of the Wall Houses that Hejduk has explored since the end of the 1960s[21] – a blind wall that hides the living to thus be able to revive it. The masks that Hejduk began to produce in the 1980s take up again the possibility of a communicative opening to the exterior. As masks they occlude, they hide, but as fantastic animals they recover the will to communicate with the city in an alternative manner. Such duality between concealment and communication seems to also exist in the cave house. Although the O'Gormans withdrew to the neighbourhood of the Pedregal, isolated from the rest of the world, their house appeared at the same time as the continued affirmation of life, and therefore, of its communion with the land.

O'Gorman's mask also shares with Hejduk a particular biomorphism. Either as a common animal or as an undefined animated creature, the mask becomes a being that inhabits the territory but at the same time is being inhabited: a collapse between an inhabitant and the dwelling that promises a reconciliation between the city and architecture. The sensation of biomorphism or sometimes anthropomorphism is present in other O'Gorman's work preceding the cave house. After his visit to the houses of Diego and Frida, with their strict

19 — The piece is titled *Part of Manhattan with Central Park, Rockefeller Center and Lincoln Center removed.* Produced at the turn of the 1960s and 1970s as part of Lewitt's cut-outs series, it was not exhibited until 1978.

20 — I am referring to Theodore Adorno's *Negative Dialectics*, an epistemology of negation to judge reality. Theodore W. Adorno, *Negative Dialectics*, E. B Ashton (trans.) (New York: Continuum, 1973). This has been used by some scholars, such as Michael Hays, to access specific architectural production of the 1960s and 1970s.

21 — The Wall Houses (1968–74) were a series of speculative architectural proposals developed by John Hejduk in continuation with the ideas he previously explored in Diamond Houses. Wall House 2, also know as the Bye House, was built in Groningen, Holland, one year after his death, in 2001. For some critics the construction of the house betrayed the strength of Hejduk's original proposal, restrained to a drawing. To see the Wall Houses as described by Hejduk in the intellectual context see: John Hejduk and Kim Shkapich, *Mask of Medusa: Works, 1947–1983* (New York: Rizzoli, 1985), 57–77.

[Figure 12] John Hejduk, *Casa para un Músico* (*House for a Musician*), 1983. For Hejduk the idea of a mask has a double significance. On the one hand, it is a *device* or an implement that hides the face. The mask negates a person with respect to the collective, and thus, an individual who wears it can make fun of the formalities and codifications of daily life. On the other hand, the mask is understood as masquerade, installation, decoration or cavalcade carriage. Hejduk unifies both meanings in a single concept that fulfils both functions: the mask hides the inhabitant and retains him and, at the same time, installs inhabitable settings. Through this carnavalesque technology, the uninhibited individual transfers his ability to inhabit to the mask, and the mask is personified or animalized in order to inhabit the city. Just as with the *palio* or the Chinese dragon, the mask inhabits the city at the request of the individual who occupies it. **Photo: Siegfried Büker.**

[Figure 13] The library of the National Autonomous University of Mexico by Juan O'Gorman, in collaboration with Gustavo Saavedra and Juan Martínez de Velasco (1949–52): a building that O'Gorman would later criticize for being a disjointed hybrid of the Internationalist architecture (that at the time was being erected extensively in Mexico) and his newly adopted organic ideal. In spite of the fact that O'Gorman ultimately reduced his participation to the elaboration of the mosaics, the building follows in sections the separation of the three pre-Hispanic worlds included in the Anahuacalli: the underworld – of onyx – on the lower floor, that in this case also controls the sun in the reading room, the earthly world in the main body of the edifice and the terrace looking at the mountain deities (just as in the Anahucalli), which with the two large mosaic eyes at the top, gives the building a humanoid appearance. **Photo: Francisco González de Canales.**

modular Functionalism and moderate use of materials, Toyo Ito commented how emotional was for him the discovery of the inhabitants of each building: 'they both began to look like the figures of the two artists: Rivera, large and corpulent, with his arm on Frida's shoulder, there, full of pride'.[22] **[figure 1]** The same anthropomorphism appears in other of O'Gorman's buildings, like the central library of UNAM. **[figure 13]** At first, the building was supposed to be the sanctification of pre-Columbian knowledge, with an original design that was never erected, like a large mass with a pyramidal torso, similar perhaps to Rivera's Anahucalli. Having had this proposal rejected, because it did not fit in with the internationalist context of the rest of tall buildings (which pelota courts and a stadium eluded because of their more discreet presence), O'Gorman decided to cover the building with mosaics to tackle the sanctification. Apart from the complex iconography that render the four walls as a grand codex of pre-Hispanic and modern scientific knowledge, the library stands as a great humanoid figure, as Edward Burian has pointed out, with Tlaloc's eyes emerging from its frame and turning it into a kind of pre-Hispanic deity.[23]

22 — Toyo Ito, 'Toyo Ito descumbre a Juan O'Gorman', in *Arquine*, 10 (Winter 1999–2000), 10.

23 — Edward R. Burian, 'The Architecture of Juan O'Gorman. Dichotomy and Drift', 142–3.

In the cave house, O'Gorman's mask is made of the land itself, like the shaman masks covered with mud, branches, shells and stones, and it aspires to the rediscovery of the Náhuatl or Aztec unity of people and the earth through a sensuous ritual. The mask examines the animals, the mountains, the sun and the moon, and the mythological deities that are reflected in it through the symbol of the stone. As the Náhuatl poet expressed it: 'Whom shall I ask? Suppose that I ask the brilliant humming-bird, the emerald trembler; suppose that I question the yellow butterfly.'[24] O'Gorman himself also asked them through his attention to the mosaic as a kind of inexhaustible and continued work through which to communicate with the earth. **[figure 14]** His work is parallel to the care taken of the garden, vegetation and arrangement of the exquisite flora, managed mainly by Helen Fowler. The 'climbing plant-stone' appears, as Juan Coronel states, because if the stone is sacred

24 — 'Ninoyolnonotza', 27.

and it is the way in which the mask questions nature, the flower is the symbol of the Náhuatl paradise, the most precious fruit of the contact between human beings and nature.[25] In his *Visión de Anáhuac* (*Vision of Anáhuac*), Alfonso Reyes writes:

In all the manifestations of indigenous life, nature performed a role as important as the one that is revealed by the tales of the conquistador; ... the flowers in the gardens were the adornment of the gods and men, as well as a subtle motivation for the plastic arts and hieroglyphics.[26]

The garden that Helen Fowler designed neither has trees for shade, nor is it an orchard for growing fruit: it is a garden with the flowers in memory of the paradise described by Reyes. Helen dressed each space with flowers, including the interior rooms, and drew with fine watercolours the species she selected, trying to distinguish and tune her sensibility to each flower she choose.

We take, we disentangle the jewels – the Náhuatl poet writes – the blue flowers are woven over the yellow, that we may give them to the children. May my soul be wrapped in several flowers, may it become drunk with them, for soon I must go away.[27]

The flower was the reiterated motif in the poetry of Anáhuac because of its sensual ability of being associated with all the myths of the earth. Alfonso Reyes writes about the flower in the pre-Hispanic world of Anáhuac:

***Flower* was one of the twenty signs of the days; flower is also the sign of the noble and the precious; and, thus, it represents perfumes and drinks. It also rises from the sacrificial blood, and crowns the hieroglyphic sign of the oratory.**[28]

Stone and flowers, and their care, like an overwhelming experience that moves our senses, are central to the way in which

25 — Juan Coronel Rivera, 'Piedra Enredadera', in Mauricio López Valdés (ed.), *O'Gorman* (México DF: Grupo Financiero Bital, 1999), 211–246.

26 — *Vision of Anáhuac* is a lyrical narration which situates the reader in Mexico in 1519, before the Spaniards arrived in the area. Alfonso Reyes, 'Visión de Anáhuac (1519)', in *Obras Completas*, vol. 2 (México DF: FCE, 1962), 28.

27 — Alfonso Reyes, 'Visión de Anáhuac', 32–3.

28 — Alfonso Reyes, 'Visión de Anáhuac', 28–9.

the O'Gormans attempted to journey/gravitate towards the lost paradise.

In spite of the fact – as it has been said on several occasions – that O'Gorman's life, and especially his marriage, was tormented, it does not seem that there was sadness or negation in the O'Gormans of those years, at least not in the period between 1948–56, in which Juan O'Gorman constructed his house with his wife and lived in it.[29] What does exist is a shout of protest against modern academic formalism and against the sequestering of life with respect to the earth. Because of it, O'Gorman's practice becomes polemical and reactive, opposed to the extraordinary reality of modern Mexico that would give way to a vast, ecologically unsustainable metropolis with enormous social inequalities. The invocation of Náhuatl spirituality, through which O'Gorman primarily carries out this protest, is established through a poetic art that connects the act of inhabitation and the building itself through the flower and the mosaic. This is a poetic art in which the world itself appears as a luscious garden of flowers and fragrances, in which one can recreate oneself by means of a long and sensuous fantasy.

It would be years later, when the clarity of the atmosphere of the valley of Mexico was lost, that Juan O'Gorman would get rid of his cave house and take refuge in his Functionalistic shell – penitent and solitary – to paint monstrous landscapes. This is how the experience of the house that Juan O'Gorman and Helen Fowler built in the foothills of the Pedregal ends, this is how 'the house of the rays of light, the house of the plumed serpents, the house of the turquoises' ceases. This is the end of the house that in the words of the poet 'shines like a multi-coloured mosaic', and from which have gone the men who 'went crying through the water'.[30] **[figure 15]**

29 — It's true that O'Gorman and Fowler moved away from the public life to devote themselves to the testing of the house project. It is also true that from 1957 the relationship between them worsened, and they ended up divorcing, remarrying and divorcing again, although they never stopped being together. Testimonies from Angela Gurría, Dolores Olmedo and Alejandro Von Wareber certify that at the beginning of the 1950s O'Gorman was a happy, fun, attentive and sociable person. Perhaps the excess of gaiety was what made Helen tremendously jealous, and what distanced her more and more from social circles (this is the hypothesis of Hilary Master's in *Shadows on a Wall: Juan O'Gorman and the Mural in Pátzcuaro*, Pittsburg: University of Pittsburgh Press, 2005), but the truth is that the O'Gorman house cannot in any way be considered a house of negativity, reclusion, torment or aversion against the world, as some have tried to believe. Roberto Vallarino, 'Evocación de O'Gorman. Semblanza en cinco Tiempos', in Mauricio López Valdés (ed.), *O'Gorman*, 82–115.

30 — Alfonso Reyes, 'Visión de Anáhuac', 33.

[Figure 14] Suns, moons, hoops, eyes: the house as mask takes on significance through the multiple eyes that look, not just by chance, toward the sacred mountains of Popocatepetl and Ixataccihatl. **Photo: Juan Guzmán, 1958. Manuel Tuissant Photographic Archive, Instituto de Investigaciones Estéticas, UNAM.**

[Figure 15] Juan O'Gorman wearing his hybrid mask construction made of mud, forest vegetation, flowers and coloured stones to celebrate his ritual. **Photo: Juan Guzmán, 1958. Manuel Tuissant Photographic Archive, Instituto de Investigaciones Estéticas, UNAM.**

A Stay Outside

Scenes of Puck*
and Analogous Architectures

Alison and Peter Smithson, Upper Lawn Solar Pavilion, Fonthill, England 1959–82

* The scenes of Puck refer to the book by Rudyard Kipling *Puck of Pook's Hill* (Cornwall: Stratus Books, 2009; first edition, 1906), a children's story that combines nearly all of the British rural myths. The article is developed based on a commentary by Professor Rafael González Sandino, that gave rise to the reading of the Smithsons' Upper Lawn Solar Pavilion through Kipling's text.

Puck, the green man, the elf that has always been there and has the same flesh as nature: Simon, one of the Smithsons' children, dressed up as the mythical green man of the English countryside in the Solar Pavilion. **Courtesy of the Smithson Family Collection, London.**

A version of this text was first published in *DC* 10-11, Barcelona, 2004. I would like to thank Junta de Andalucia for the institutional support, and for the help and comments of my colleagues: José Ramón Moreno Pérez, Mariano Pérez Humanes, Rafael Sandino, Paolo Sustertic and HUM-711 research group form the Universtity of Seville.

For decades the knowledge of twentieth century architecture has developed in a fundamentally endogenous form, which has given way to conspicuous criticism of architectural facts, even though the formulation of its history has remained generally incomplete. From the wholehearted applause of the first critics of the Modern Movement (Henry-Russell Hitchcock, Sigfried Gideon, Nikolaus Pevsner, J. M. Richards or Bruno Zevi), to revisionisms, irony, disqualification and today's perplexity about the present condition, architecture has never stopped looking at itself, or even worse, has never stopped looking only at its heroes. As a consequence, it has lost an opportunity to actively incorporate values that are external to it, where the majority of the issues that really affect contemporary life are found. Today we can say that the internal disciplinary criticism of modern architecture, produced from inside the Modern Movement, has become rather superfluous, and that its new revisions and bifurcations will never stop to be so until they begin to evaluate architectural facts from the viewpoint of relevance to a society that receives them: a society whose fundamental features are dispersion, fragmentation and diversity, as is the plurality of forms of life that this society accommodates. As opposed to the endogenous reading that has characterized architectural disciplinary criticism for so many years, the exogenous reading starts with the supposition of a lack of consensus and, therefore, of the impossibility of the *a priori* organization and division of knowledge. Without a stable ground to inquire from, the only possibility of understanding architectural facts is the collection of confrontations with *the other* – that is, with instruments, knowledge and practices that are exterior to it.[1]

1 — This way of understanding architectural criticism was part of the intense debates with José Ramón Moreno Pérez at the University of Seville in the years 2002–4. These early discussion about the exogenous reading of architecture and its relationship with society can be found in our articles of the period. See for instance: José Ramón Moreno Pérez,

'Impacto Maximo, Obsolescencia Inmediata: Re-Ciclaje. Anotaciones para un Metapanorama de Arquitectura Contemporánea', in *Arquitectura,* 336 (2004), 20–27, and Francisco González de Canales, 'Ampliación del Campo de Batalla', in *Metalocus,* 12/13 (2003), 108–119. Some of these issues appeared in the PhD seminar *Objetos para ser destruidos, el lugar de las cosas (mercancías, habitación, identidad),* ETSA de Sevilla, March–April 2003, led by José Ramón Moreno and Mariano Pérez-Humanes.

One of the research fields that has tried to establish such exogenous readings of a discipline is the so-known cultural studies. At the beginning of the 1980s any discipline of knowledge seemed to end up being subsumed by the society, and as a response to this phenomenon taking place in the cultural sphere, the field of cultural studies erupted. Upon an apparent freeing of the masses from the impositions of a vertically administered culture, the elitist, closed spheres of knowledge appeared to be contested by the social, either in the scientific fields (just as Bruno Latour tried to demonstrate) or in ethics, philosophy, technology, anthropology, literature and, of course, in architecture. Perhaps cultural studies, as Fredric Jameson suggests, are more a symptom than a true theoretical wager, an illness that we have half-diagnosed and for which we do not yet have a cure;[2] or maybe, as Raymond Williams affirmed at the beginning of the 1980s, it is nowadays the more specialized way of working within the human sciences.[3]

While it is true that we can speak of cultural studies beyond the Anglo-Saxon academia, with outstanding examples such as the work of the literary critic Ángel Rama in the Spanish-speaking world, an inevitable tendency exists to see cultural studies as a purely Anglo-Saxon invention. It was fundamentally introduced in the Spanish-speaking and other academic contexts through the incorporation of Raymond Williams's work,[4] and less so that of Leo Marx,[5] and in general, by an alternative reading of what until then had been called sociology of culture – a field that attempted to unite Mikhail Bakhtin's polyphony, writings of Walter Benjamin and some of Pierre Bourdieu's works. In any case, the centrality of Raymond Williams in any aspect of the development of the field seems undeniable. On the one hand, Williams's radical historicism

2 — Fredric Jameson and Slavoj Žižek, *Estudios Culturales. Reflexiones sobre el multiculturalismo* (Buenos Aires: Paidós, 1998), 69–136.
3 — Raymond Williams, *The Sociology of Culture* (Chicago: University of Chicago Press, 1981), 9–32.
4 — His most influential works would be the political revision of the artistic avant-gardes in *The Politics of Modernism: Against the New Conformists* (London, New York: Verso, 1989), and his more ambitious program of cultural sociology in *Culture and Society, 1780–1950* [Harmondsworth: Penguin, 1971 (1958)]. In my study I am most concerned with the fundamental text *The Country and the City* (New York: Oxford University Press, 1973).
5 — See his very influential work on pastoralism in American literature: Leo Marx, *The Machine in the Garden: Technology and the Pastoral Ideal in America* [New York/London: Oxford University Press, 1972 (1964)].

permits a criticism of the structuralist and post-structuralist tendencies of the 1970s and 1980s, through which French Marxist thought was rebuilt after May 68. On the other, Williams proposes an alternative to the structuralist Marxism, trapped by a radical criticism of experience, which after Louis Althusser's critique of ideology had paralyzed any type of historical reading of social configurations.[6] As is known, in Althusser's theorization, the fields of science and ideology were once and for all separate, a perception which actively dismantled the interaction between culture and society, trapped since then in the mirror of ideology.[7] Raymond Williams's alternative is therefore presented as a way of returning to making a positive criticism that extends from minor customs and practices, from our daily life and its means of expression, to the central questions of society in relation to culture.[8] Williams's reading thus proposes a re-interweaving of the cultural, the social and the political: a return to the battlefield that the poststructuralist criticism tried to squander in recent decades. As he remarks in the *Politics of Modernism:*

If we are to break out of the non-historical fixity of *post*-modernism, then we must search out and counterpose an alternative tradition taken from the neglected works left in the wide margin of the century, a tradition which may address itself not to this by now exploitable because quite inhuman rewriting of the past but, for all our sakes, to a modern *future* in which community can be imagined again.[9]

While it is true that in the 1980s and 1990s the theory and criticism of architecture were obsessed with poststructuralist discourses, it does not mean

6 — An account of the importance of Raymond Williams's work in contraposition to the work of the most influential French structuralist and poststructuralist philosophers of that time can be found in: Beatriz Sarlo, 'Raymond Williams: una relectura', in Mabel Moraña (ed.), *Nuevas perspectivas desde/sobre América Latina: El desafío de los estudios culturales* (Santiago de Chile: Cuarto Propio, 2000).

7 — The circle formed by Althusser, Lacan and Barthes would be trapped by this mirror, that would grow with the publication *Tel Quel* as a new theoretic academic vade mecum. Althusser takes Jacques Lacan's theory of the mirror stage, used by many theoreticians of architecture for a criticism of the expropriation of the imaginary, as a frame that limits us in our way of looking and our imagination. In Althusser ideology is like the mirror in which one seeks to recognize oneself, but that by itself has no positive or negative value (as Georg Lukács or Benjamin and, in general, Marxism before 1968, including Manfredo Tafuri, believed). It is the only thing between the world and our reality, which operate in different spheres that don t touch each other. Ideology is the only frame within which we move, the mirror in which we discover ourselves, but if we break it, we break ourselves with it. Nothing can remain outside of the mirror. In a certain way this attitude will become conservative and that is the criticism that Raymond Williams makes. See Louis Althusser, 'Ideology and Ideological: State Apparatus (Notes Towards an Investigation)', in *Lenin and Philosophy and Other Essays* (London: New Left Books, 1977), 85 ff.

8 — Already in his very early 'Culture is Ordinary', Williams makes reference to the central role of the most ordinary practices of daily life to the understanding of what culture means nowadays. See Raymond Williams, 'Culture is Ordinary', in *Resources of Hope: Culture, Democracy, Socialism* (London: Verso, 1989), 37–48.

that architecture had not previously tried to tackle the questions of cultural studies raised by Williams. On the contrary, exemplary and pioneering practices have always existed within our discipline, perhaps one of the most memorable being those of Manfredo Tafuri and his incipient interdisciplinary approach at the turn of the 1960s and 1970s. During those years the Roman theoretician tried to understand – in a radical criticism that joined culture, politics and sociology – the implications of the architecture typical of his time and what it formulation meant in his present society.[10] Guided by complex interpretative structures, Tafuri registered that the discovery of an exogenous explanation of architectural facts would bring as a consequence a structural change in the understanding of architecture as a form of knowledge, and therefore, a fundamental displacement within the discipline itself. As he pointed out in *Architecture and Utopia,* it was a necessary move, capable of assimilating the new problems the world was facing (be it ecology, mass culture or heritage), not just to be able to continue moving forward but rather in order to correct the steps that had already been taken (or as Habermas writes, 'to plan the legacy' for a dehumanized society).[11] Using the more recent and polemical tone of Peter Sloterdijk, it would not only be a matter of building the present but rather of realizing the fundamental task of man to transmit his past life through ephemeral affinities and friendships within the logic and philology of global language.[12]

My text forms part of the group of initiatives attempting to balance the endogenous reading of architecture with another, exogenous reading – that is, it tries to tackle architecture from the outside of the discipline. In this case, I approach modern architecture from the perspective of its confrontation with nature and material culture of the English rural tradition. In the following passages, I employ

9 — *The Politics of Modernism: Against the New Conformists,* 35.

10 — Some of the outstanding texts of Tafuri were 'Towards a Critique of Architectural Ideology' and 'L'Architecture dans le Boudoir', in which he critically reads the architecture of the time using critical theory of Georg Lukács and Walter Benjamin, and making interdisciplinary jumps. This type of approach to criticism will be followed by Josep Quetglas and his colleagues. Manfredo Tafuri: 'Towards a Critique of Architectural Ideology' and 'L'Architecture dans le Boudoir' in K. Michael Hays (ed.), *Architectural Theory since 1968* (Cambridge, MA: MIT Press, 1998), 2–35 and 146–72 (first publication in Italian in 1969 and 1974, respectively).

11 — Manfredo Tafuri, *Architecture and Utopia: Design and Capitalist Development,* Barbara Luigia La Penta (trans.), (Cambridge, MA: MIT Press, 1976). (Italian version published first in Bari by Laterza in 1973.)

12 — Peter Sloterdijk, *En el mismo barco. Ensayo sobre la hiperpolítica* (Madrid: Siruela, 1994), 8 ff. Sloterdijk reviews the human political structures and tries to take advantage of the current break within the common consensus around the Enlightenment project, so that he can reconnect the originary principle of the human tribal communities with the current *hyper-political* order.

the strict relationship of this tradition with the flow of the everyday life. Hence, my reading of Alison and Peter Smithson's work does not consist of appropriately binding their projects with the lineages and preoccupations of the great modern architectures (by which they were, without any doubt, enormously influenced); rather I trace signs in images, analyze apparently insignificant everyday practices or intertwine fragments of diverse stories, capable of bringing us closer to the complex cultural framework that surrounds the Smithsons' form of life in their Solar Pavilion. To carry out this exogenous reading, I have looked to literary support: to Rudyard Kipling's *Puck of Pook's Hill,* which will take us deep into the cosmology of the rural English culture.[13] Therefore, this investigation begins in the heart of rural England, between the novelist Kipling and the architects Alison and Peter Smithson; between the imaginary and the sensible, understood as a way of inhabiting that extends to an entire territory.[14]

Rural England

The idea of the countryside in England is laden with many fantasies and idealizations since its lands were violated through intensive industrialization earlier than anywhere else.[15] In England, perhaps with more force than in any other place in Europe, there has always been the need to produce a scenography and iconography typical of the countryside, creating what Raymond Williams calls a 'structure of feeling', or horizon of imaginary possibilities, around everything rural. This phenomenon is exemplified by enduring literary concepts and social experiences. Hence, the construction of this imaginary also consists of an ongoing evolution of cultural languages associated with all that is rural, in which certain ideas or stereotypes are repeated in very diverse forms.[16]

One of the oldest and most robust sentiments of the English rural tradition is the antagonism between

13 — Alison and Peter Smithson had demonstrated an interest in different interpretations of rural England for children and Alison Smithson text on Beatrix Potter illustrations is a paradigmatic example of this. Alison Smithson, 'Beatrix Potter's Places', in *Architectural Design* (Dec. 1967), 573–30.

14 — The book unfolds in the county of Sussex, in the south of England, known for its rural isolation in comparison with other regions of the country.

15 — Of course, the Industrial Revolution began in England, invading not only the cities but also British countryside, with factories scattered across the rural landscape. In novels such as Mary Shelley's *Frankenstein* (1816) or Robert Louis Stevenson's *The Strange Case of Dr. Jekyll and Mr. Hyde* (1886), we clearly see this type of guilt – the dark side of science that is produced by violating Nature.

16 — The concept 'structure of feeling', which is quite consistent in Raymond Williams's work, appears for the first time in *The Long Revolution* and it is also used in *The Country and the City* to approach the English rural culture. Raymond Williams, *The Long Revolution* (Toronto: Broadview Press, 2001), 64–6; and Raymond Williams, *The Country and the City* (New York: Oxford University Press, 1973), 4–8.

life in the country and life in the city, and a belief in a golden era when there was a perfect harmony between people and their land.[17] The sense of loss in relation to the golden age becomes more acute in the modern period, but – according to Williams – it can be traced back to antiquity and, especially, to what we know as the pastoral poetry developed in the Hellenic period by Theocritus and Hesiod. The same pastoralism had a strong impact on the British aristocracy from the seventeenth century onwards, also in the sophisticated manners of what Williams called the counter-pastoral movement – a poetic mood in which we can observe the profound breach between what is being described and the actual way of peasant life in the country during this time, depicted nonetheless without a particular will of idealization. It is also when the concept of *landscape* is born in England through a type of observer who has removed himself from the world of labour.[18]

17 — Raymond Williams, *The Country and the City*, 46–54.
18 — Raymond Williams, *The Country and the City*, 13–35.

Beyond this infamous antagonism between the country and the city, British literature also seems to register another subtle difference in life of the two realms. This is what we find in the writings of Charles Dickens or Thomas Hardy, to mention two examples emphasized by Williams. In popular imagination and in British literature, the great city, as opposed to the countryside, makes life's successes imperceptible with respect to the spaces in which the life takes place. Therefore, life in the city always appears to create a rupture with a type of rural community, recognizable by its own, smaller group of members.[19] The ideology of the goodness of the countryside in contrast with the corruption of the city appears to be strongly rooted in the popular British imagination, as is indicated by the fact that the advance of the modern age was frequently accompanied by a major demand for the iconography and expressions typical of everything rural (at least until the middle of the twentieth century).[20] In fact, in the British post-war cultural climate, ideas of progress based on machinery and industrial development had their compensation in a

19 — Something similar happened later in Germany, and it would be the motivation for study by the most important social thinkers of the beginning of the century, like Ferdinand Tonnies or George Simmel. It would also underlie the thinking of Georg Lukács and Walter Benjamin.
20 — To a large extent, the New Towns that appeared during the post-war reconstruction would have many of the components of the rural imaginary in its most crude and superficial sense.

strong interest in the national identity, reflected in a growing recovery of themes originating in the British rural culture. Such a strange combination could be observed in the Festival of Britain, celebrated in London in 1951, in which ingenious technological artefacts and industrially advanced architecture mixed with exaggerated recreations of campestral myths and a range of bucolic motifs – to the great delight of the working classes.[21] The exaltation of rural England that emerged in the post-war period was still present in the Smithsons' intellectual preoccupations in the 1950s, which maintained a clear interest in the tastes of the lower classes. This is also evident in their use of images by Nigel Henderson – of children playing in Bethnal Green, a working-class neighbourhood – in their presentation of the *Urban Re-Identification Grid* to the International Congress for Modern Architecture (CIAM) of 1953.[22] Through the tastes of the lower and middle classes, the Smithsons planned to create a new community model based on a specific material culture, in which authenticity and a shared sense of values would still be possible.[23] In the mid-1950s this idea became even more important for the British duo as a specific desire to recover modest rural architectural patterns for the purpose of generating new communities. This was announced in The Doorn Manifesto (1954), which reclaimed ideas of the innovative biologist Patrick Geddes about the relationship between community and territory at a topological level. Through journeys, some by car, the Smithsons intuitively threw themselves into the conquest of this new landscape, as yet unexplored by the dominant culture. Diverse excursions into this territory and importations from the countryside to the city produced modest proposals, such

21 — The Festival of Britain was staged as a post-Second World War celebration to raise the morale of the British citizens, as the country at the beginning of the 1950s was still living in semi-ruins and was subject to ration books. The exhibition was a highly indulgent, populist event, and it is fundamental to understanding of the culture of the English masses. It's interesting to note a unique occurrence in England in which the pastoral demand on the part of the aristocracy in the seventeenth century is absorbed by the lower classes to the point of forming an inherent part of the lower classes' identity by the end of the nineteenth century. It was also reflected in the dispersion from the city to the periphery, which had begun with the aristocracy, but by the end of the nineteenth century was a movement by the working class. Becky E. Conekin, *The Autobiography of a Nation: The 1951 Festival of Britain* (Manchester: Manchester University Press, 2003).

22 — Alison and Peter Smithson were the rare individuals of the working-class origin who had managed to slip into the upper cultural spheres. Social classes in England continued to be of major importance in the post-war years – something that really didn't occur in the United States. The introduction of working class material culture and tastes was one of the battles of the groups that didn't belong to the traditional, dominant high class – like the Independent Group – that took their example from the socialization of the culture of the United States as a reference. It is interesting to see in the testimony of some of the American architects who traveled to England to study during the 1960s (like George Baird or Peter Eisenman), how deeply shocking for them was the class structuring of the British society.

23 — The term authenticity, taken from Jean-Paul Sartre's existentialism, and the idea of belonging, based on the sentimental association of a community, were fundamental for the Smithsons during the 1950s. See, for instance, Sarah Williams Goldhagen, 'Freedom's Domiciles', in Sarah Williams Goldhagen and Réjean Legault (eds.), *Anxious Modernisms* (Cambridge, MA: MIT Press, 2001), 74–95.

[Figure 1] Wayland Young Pavilion in Bayswater, London, which Alison and Peter Smithson (1959–82) developed in parallel to the Solar Pavilion.

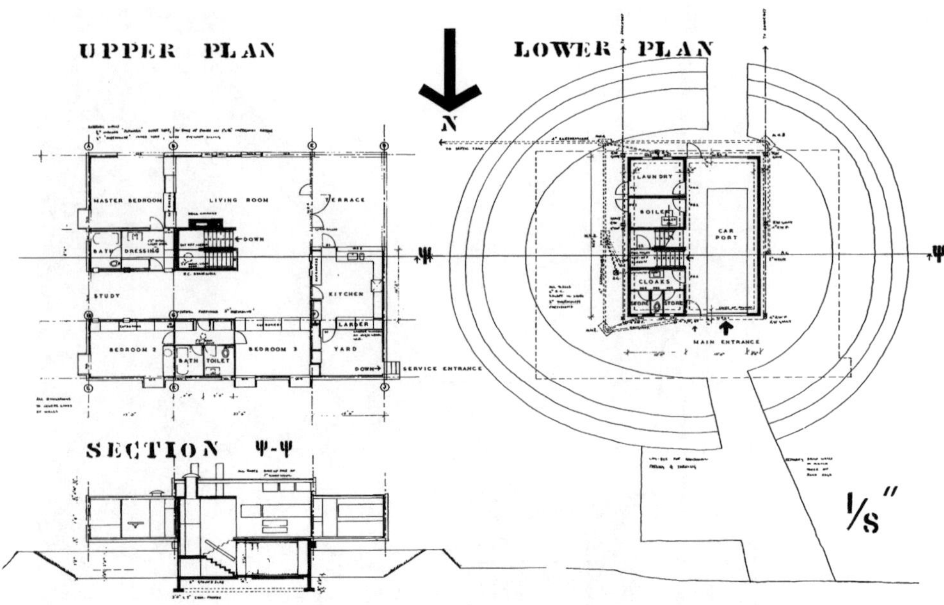

[Figure 2] Bate's Burrows Lea Farm in Shere (1953–5) presented at CIAM X in Dubrovnik. The Smithsons proposed this dwelling as a model of an isolated settlement, as their rereading of Patrick Geddes's 'valley section'. Modern architecture had worked with social dwelling, public building and perhaps factories and offices, but few times had it approached the rural world in such a specific way. The building creates a subtle parapet that the Smithsons had found in several rural English buildings and that embeds the farm into the orchard landscape that surrounds it. **The Alison and Peter Smithson Archive. Frances Loeb Library, Harvard Graduate School of Design.**

[Figure 3] Preparatory panels for the Galleon Cottages for the International Congress of Modern Architecture (CIAM) X in Dubrovnik, where Alison and Peter Smithsons' studies of the rural English architecture were shown. The cottages' relationship with the landscape, their structure and their topographic position follow the ideas of Patrick Geddes. In the upper panel the Smithsons describe as an outrage the architecture of the New Towns that were being planned in England at that time, countering it with the strong relationship between architecture and landscape of the traditional settlements, shown on the right. In the lower image they depict a traditional settlement in Brainbridge, with its sinuous adaptation to the forms of the valley and its relationship with the agricultural lands that support it.

galleon
cottages
OUTRAGE
the tradition
1

2
BAINBRIDGE

as Bate's Burrows Lea Farm in Shere or the Galleon Cottages in Hamlet (1953–5), both of which were presented at the CIAM X in Dubrovnik; the small work at Bark Place Mews in London (1953–6); the Sugden House in Watford (1955–1956); the sketches for the English Climate House (1957) and the Wayland Young Pavilion in Bayswater (1959–82) **[figure 1]**. In other words, an entire series of works from 1953 to 1959 outlined an approach to English rural culture from different angles, accompanied by sketches and photographic reports that are today preserved in the archives of the Frances Loeb Library at the Harvard University. **[figures 2 and 3]** The culmination of this process was the construction of the Solar Pavilion in Fonthill. That is where the Smithsons tested the myth of the English countryside that had so captivated them with 'the freely chosen isolation'[24] it represented – in contrast with the noise and the 'sensation of invaded territory' (i.e., the city, urbanization). So, from time to time, Alison and Peter Smithson with their children withdrew from the city to an ephemeral-looking pavilion, where they attempted to 'establish a territory under their own control'.[25] They felt that the new order of their lives would be compatible with the small everyday things: the mutual belonging of the human, the natural, the memories and imagination. **[figure 4]**

24 — Peter Smithson, 'Introduction', in Alison and Peter Smithson, *Upper Lawn: Folly Solar Pavilion,* Enric Miralles (intro.), (Barcelona: Ediciones de la Universitat Politècnica de Catalunya, 1986).

25 — Ibid.

Puck of Pook's Hill

Within English literature, Kipling's *Puck of Pook's Hill* is a unique example of a subtle reflection on the country's rural culture. Perhaps it just turned out that way precisely because the author never meant to create a book about English rural life but rather a history of England for children, which would intertwine with the life of two little kids in the county of Sussex. Yet, with his story Kipling opened a window onto the mythical England, with Puck himself as the presenter. The children, Dan and Una, give life to the book, seeing in their own home on Pook's Hill, in the stream, the blacksmith's workshop or the Linden's farm, the most fantastic apparitions of Roman centurions and medieval knights as if the past and present were melded into one.

[Figure 4] Upper Lawn Folly Solar Pavilion (1959–82) on a summer day. The pavilion was born with the intention of creating a prototype of a climatic dwelling for a specific location in England. Resting on a massive wall facing north and trying to gain as much solar energy as possible from the south (and somewhat less on the east and west sides), the dwelling attempts to optimize the gains and losses of energy in a natural way. The Smithsons made several excursions into the countryside: they and their children had travelled all over; they had drawn and they had photographed several places before they were captivated by this small enclave on a farm in Fonthill. What began as a climatic experiment ended up being an in-depth study of the English rural world, its myths and its way of life, its distinct temporality and its sensory experiences. **Courtesy of the Smithson Family Collection, London.**

The importance of life in consonance with the land is not a banal issue in England. The territory, or 'these lands' as Puck says, is charged with life, years, noises and mystery. It is a condensation and compaction of history all over the ground of the experienced territory. As in old convents, where the gravestones that living people walk on safeguard the dead, here the land is made up of life and death, of instances of memory and oblivion. **[figure 5]** Puck's territory is thus spatially and temporally defined all at once.[26] The 'Puck's Song' says:

See you the dimpled track that runs,
All hollow through the wheat?
O that was where they hauled the guns
That smote King Philip's fleet!
See you our little mill that clacks,
So busy by the brook?
She has ground her corn and paid her tax
Ever since Domesday Book.
See you our stilly woods of oak,
And the dread ditch beside?
O that was where the Saxons broke,
On the day that Harold died!
Trackway and Camp and City lost,
Salt Marsh where now is corn;
Old Wars, old Peace, old Arts that cease,
And so was England born![27]

When Puck says '*you see this path*', the one where the cannons that defeated King Phillip were placed, he is referring to a path that is right there, that exists today and that we can still follow the same way the 'heroic victors' did. The same occurs in the case of the old mill and the oak forests. They are still there and they live with us. Puck explains this territory to us in such a way that England's memory is alive in everything we see, in every single place. However, this memory that pervades all senses cannot be recalled in a linear manner. Already at the beginning of the book,

26 — Kipling's entire text is peppered with references to popular songs, poems and stories that are well known in England.

27 — Rudyard Kipling, *Puck of Pook's Hill* (Cornwall: Stratus Books, 2009), 3.

[Figure 5] Paving of Alison and Peter Smithsons' Solar Pavilion. The marks in the stone contain the history of the place: the erosion of footsteps; paving modified for the entrance; placement of the drain; the mark of the old boundary of the farm. **Courtesy of the Smithson Family Collection, London.**

in the 'Song of Puck', the facts being noted do not coincide with a linear historical succession. Time is backwards. From the era of Henry VIII, through the Norman invasion, the Saxon kings, Britannia, prehistoric England and up to Merlin the magician, everything is part of the process of enchantment in which the past and the present are inverted.[28] For that reason, I will close this chapter only by referring to certain particular scenes in illustrations, to the images captured in time, that now coexist with our present.

Puck charms us through the dissolution of the barrier between memory and experience. He does it to us the same way he does it to Dan and Una, the children who are the protagonists of the story, opening and closing our memory, shaking ash leaves and the thorn tree. The two oldest beings in England, even older than Puck himself, the ash and thorn trees are the two symbolic governors of this remembrance/oblivion, of the life in harmony with nature and the past. **[see page 145]** Thus, we share with this elf from *A Midsummer Night's Dream* the search for a form of life close to the myth, an alternative world that Shakespeare himself vindicates with the words of Hippolyta:

But all the story of the night told over,
And all their minds transfigured so together,
More witnesseth than fancy's images
And grows to something of great constancy;
But, howsoever, strange and admirable.[29]

Scenes of Puck[30]

The following epigraphs describe the complex of spaces in which the children live (Dan and Una/Simon and Samantha Smithson), and that define a domestic terrain: scenes taken from Kipling's description of rural England, on the one hand, and photographs taken by Alison and Peter Smithson from 1959 to 1982, on the other. These are fragments of life stolen from time, immortalized in their present, which inaugurate a new way of inhabitation, stemming from the proposal of a voluntarily isolation.

28 — This alteration, in which the temporal order is inverted, is a device employed brilliantly by Alejo Carpentier in his story *Viaje a la semilla*. Carpentier's story is quoted in Josep Quetglas, 'La danza y la procesión', in *El Croquis* 64, 26–45.

29 — William Shakespeare, 'Midsummer Night's Dream', in *The Complete Works of William Shakespeare* (Wordsworth Library Collection), 297.

30 — The seven epigraphs are equivalent to seven of the ten chapters of the Kipling's book. Missing are the second, fourth, seventh and ninth, which I considered to be of a lesser importance to the ends of my chapter.

The theatre in the stable

'The Children were at the Theatre, acting to Three Cows as much as they could remember of Midsummer Night's Dream. ... The Theatre lay in a meadow called the Long Slip. A little mill-stream, carrying water to a mill two or three fields away, bent round one corner of it, and in the middle of the bend lay a large old Fairy Ring of darkened grass, which was the stage. The mill-stream banks, overgrown with willow, hazel, and guelder-rose, made convenient places to wait in till your turn came; and a grown-up who had seen it said that Shakespeare himself could not have imagined a more suitable setting for his play.

... Three Cows had been milked and were grazing steadily with a tearing noise that one could hear all down the meadow; and the noise of the Mill at work sounded like bare feet running on hard ground. A cuckoo sat on a gate-post singing his broken June tune, 'cuckoo-cuck', while a busy kingfisher crossed from the mill-stream, to the brook which ran on the other side of the meadow. Everything else was a sort of thick, sleepy stillness smelling of meadow-sweet and dry grass.'[31]

The children's play is interrupted by Puck, whose imaginative tale of the history of England melds with the children's performance in the stable. It all occurs in the same space, where the imaginary and the sensible are combined into one.

Courtesy of the Smithson Family Collection, London.

31 — Rudyard Kipling, ibid., 5–6.

The boat and the brook

'It was too hot to run about in the open, so Dan asked their friend, old Hobden, to take their own dinghy from the pond and put her on the brook at the bottom of the garden. Her painted name was the Daisy, but for exploring expeditions she was the Golden Hind or the Long Serpent, or some such suitable name. Dan hiked and howked with a boat-hook (the brook was too narrow for sculls), and Una punted with a piece of hop-pole. When they came to a very shallow place (the Golden Hind drew quite three inches of water) they disembarked and scuffled her over the gravel by her towrope, and when they reached the overgrown banks beyond the garden they pulled themselves upstream by the low branches.'[32]

In the midst of the navigational difficulties, Sir Richard Drake appears, a gentleman crusader, who narrates the story of the Danish adventurers, who sometimes disembarked on the shores of England. Once again the children's sailing melds with the story of Sir Richard, who tells of his voyage with a group of Danes to the unknown lands, where he met demons and beings that he could not even describe. It is the world of the unknown, of that which still does not have a name. The children also participate in this world through their continuous discovery via navigation. To investigate and to know what is one's own become one and the same experience.

Courtesy Smithson Family Collection, London.

32 — Ibid., 37.

A forest with a door

While yet our England was wolfish den;
Before our forests heard the talk of men
JOHN KEATS, 'ENDYMION'

'Una slipped through their private gap in the fence, and sat still awhile, scowling as scowlily and lordlily as she knew how.'[33] The children call this place Volaterrae because of the verse from the *Lays of Ancient Rome* by Thomas Babbington Macaulay, which are well known in England.[34] In their coming and going, the little girl detects a movement in the undergrowth, and a treacherous gust uncovers a strangely dressed man, hidden behind a thorn tree (the thorn tree which is the protector of English tradition). 'They call me Parnesius. I have been a Centurion of the Seventh Cohort of the Thirtieth Legion — the Ulpia Victrix.'[35] Parnesius recounts that Volaterrae was a great watchtower beyond the faraway forest. The door of the forest was the passageway to a great road that connected the northern and the southern parts of the province and made it possible to cross the woods that otherwise would be easy to get lost in. Parnesius' and the children's forest is a tame one, *a forest with a door*. Hence, current life space – with the hill at the end of the forest and the door in the hedge – is completed by the world that Parnesius has appeared from in front of the children. And everything closes in the same setting that they inhabit every day.

Courtesy of the Smithson Family Collection, London.

33 — Ibid., 74.
34 — 'From lordly Volaterrae,/Where scowls the far-famed hold/Piled by the hands of giants/For Godlike Kings of old.' Baron Thomas Babbington Macaulay, *Lays of Ancient Rome*, quoted in Rudyard Kipling, 101.
35 — Kipling, ibid., 75.

The great wall

The great wall is the boundary of the territory. Parnesius goes back to describe the territory as a voyage, as something that is being understood while it is being crossed: point by point, from side to side. As we approach the boundary, everything becomes more arid, things begin to lack names. 'You fetch clear of the forests and climb bare hills, where wolves howl in the ruins of our cities that have been. No more pretty girls; no more jolly magistrates who knew your Father when he was young, and invite you to stay with them; no news at the temples and way stations except bad news of wild beasts. There's where you meet hunters, and trappers for the Circuses, prodding along chained bears and muzzled wolves. Your pony shies at them, and your men laugh.'[36] The territory becomes the negative of what we previously described as our land. At its border a vast enclosure appears: an extraordinary limit of the unnamed, which emerges as a final chaotic accumulation of everything nameable.

Hadrian's Wall, as Kipling describes it, is a Babel of all the Roman provinces, a mixture of barbarity and a great work of Roman engineering. This Babel is longitudinal, of stone piled some ten meters high, finished off with minarets where centuries of defence have been concentrated. The wall is longer than a human eye can see: it crosses the island from coast to coast. The adjacent city is an extension of voices, of noises and people: 'houses and temples, shops and theatres, barracks and granaries, trickling along like dice behind—always behind—one long, low, rising and falling, and hiding and showing line of towers'.[37] In spite of its consistency, it is not a permanent city. It is demolished and built, depending on the boundary it offers to the exterior: *to that which has no name.* **Courtesy of the Smithson Family Collection, London.**

Between the mill and the farm

Dan and Una played pirates in the mill. 'If you don't mind rats on the rafters and oats in your shoes, the mill-attic, with its trap-doors and inscriptions on beams about floods and sweethearts, is a splendid place. It is lighted by a foot-square window, called Duck Window.'[38] It is only a few inches high and, as its name indicates, it does not seem to be a window for a man but rather for a domesticated animal. The route around the farm has a variety of gardens, pigs in a pigsty and a woman with a child in her arms. The farm is in the front, the house in the back. It seems the house is a secondary space that is barely described, because the best lighting is for the farm. The world depicted here is not only for humans: it is like the Duck Window.

In old Sussex, in the heart of rural England, to know 'these lands' is also to comprehend what seem to be accidental facts of nature. A fallen oak tree, in total collapse, is a passageway for rabbits and its roots suture together the two banks of the river, protecting the riverbed during the floods. Only old Hodben and the children know the importance of this unfortunate tree when the father prepares to cut it down. **Courtesy of the Smithson Family Collection, London.**

36 — Ibid., 78.
37 — Ibid., 90.
38 — Ibid., 118.

Epilogue

Juan José Lahuerta

Reading the book by Francisco González de Canales brings to mind a photo of the house in Vaucresson that Le Corbusier built in 1922, and which is one of the first pure examples of his style of architecture. Published in the first volume of his *Complete Works*, it shows the façade looking out onto the garden: a rectangular floor plan organised by hidden layouts and crossed by two horizontal spaces: the huge window on the ground floor and the horizontal window upstairs. The frontality of the photograph exaggerates the flatness, symmetry and the suspended abstraction of this purist composition. Our eyes cannot fail to rest on it, seduced by so much elementary perfection, and in such large amounts. For this reason, there is no greater surprise than when, by one of those flukes when our eye moves involuntarily because of the strain caused by too much attention, we change focus and discover the doghouse over in the bottom on the right, under the watchful eye, incidentally, of its occupant, the only one breaking up the pertinent feeling of *absence* conveyed by the picture. As opposed to the orthogonal composition, with the horizontal window, the flat roof and the machinists' evocations of what we shall term the main building –the one designed by Le Corbusier– the little doghouse appears suddenly like a strange, unexpected miniature, with its gabled, steeply sloping roof, and arched doorway, in a position that is somewhat foreshortened. We can no longer take our eyes off it. Such is the effect of photography that, once the spatial and symbolic continuity of the old perspective has been broken, even the most insignificant details tend to elbow their way into the foreground, and actually scratch themselves onto our retina. However, in this case, this is not the only thing. There is something even more important and it is the following: whereas in the main house what we recognise is the classic or purist style attributable to Le Corbusier, in the kennel what we see – and feel – is the house, or more to the point, its archetype. The main building is the local and dated architectural structure designed by Le Corbusier and imitated by many over the course of a few years. On the other hand, the kennel is the universal house a child would paint, the one that would be built out of straw, wood or stone, without any concern for the materials, but definitely in that shape, by the three little pigs, or what the classic philosophers, from Filarete to Laugier, and others, would imagine to be the primitive hut. What our eyes see in it, and what ties them to it – to its roofed form, which speaks of the rain sliding down it, and its archway, which evokes the idea of a cave – is the memory of our true origin and real refuge. It is the figure used by Filarete to represent Adam expelled from Paradise, covering his head with his hands to form a roof; or the way Laugier portrays the famous hut, erected not with wooden spears but on top of deep rooted trees, whose branches support the sloping gables of the roof; like that hut on stilts erected by Robinson Crusoe, which he built to protect himself from wild animals, whose stakes take root and bloom in the springtime. How is it that Le Corbusier, who had no trouble at all removing anything that annoyed him in his photos, left it there? We won't go into that now. At the end of the day, it is the dog's house and he is right there, as I said, standing opposite the archway, looking so brazen and so alert, the guardian of the archetypal building. No, the book by Francisco González de Canales, which the reader has in their hands, is not about the main building, as we might think or be expected to think, but of the dog kennel, or at least, of *that* little dog's house we see here and which holds our gaze without letting go. What I want to say is that your attention is not directed to the posthumous, forever frosty architecture of modernity but to a different type of architecture, that smacks of domestic emergency and self-experimentation, which, like what happens in the case of DIY, is based on never-ending experience and, as González de Canales himself makes perfectly clear, sets itself up as an 'alternative product' finding a way in under the guise of 'civil development'. Although in the cases he is concerned with – and this needs to be kept firmly in mind – the rules of the game have changed beyond all recognition with respect to the myths of yesteryear that I mentioned above – Filarete, Laugier, Crusoe or the three little pigs and their longing for permanent masonry. The purpose of the archetypal building – this is spelled out quite clearly in this book – is not in its cyclical union with Nature, in its identification with her as a beginning and end, where the work of humanity is indeed effective but merely transitory. Quite the opposite. In the *disappearance* of Nature itself in the face of a 'habitational artform' – without any telltale signs, I would reiterate once again, that it would have to be a contradiction in terms. The chronological span chosen in this book cannot, in fact, be more significant: 1937–1959, the central period, since it is the most visible – if we can describe it in those words – of the terror and dispossession that are typical of a century in which man 'has been stripped of the great outdoors'. Nature has not managed to hold on to even its name: 'the great outdoors' is a clinical certainty, in the time of medical metaphors. Another image now comes to mind, an engraving by Ledoux entitled *L'abri du pauvre*, in which we can see a small man in the nude in the shelter of a leafy tree, sitting on some hewn stones, looking up at the sky, and in the absence of a fire – or a fireplace – with the palms of his hands stretched out towards the warmth provided by the sun's rays. That primitive man is the poor devil that, without doubt, is just as harmonious as Nature – or the gods – which does not abandon him, or better still, that cannot abandon him because she is really him, and just as *primitive*. In the book by Francisco González de Canales, on the other hand, whenever the people, wrapped up inside all kinds of orthopaedic protection – starting with gas masks – looked up at the sky, they would see – and still see – jet bombers, and the comforting warmth has for them become a permanent fire: *the* fire, as the amazing book by Jörg Friedrich on the Second World War has as its simple title. There is no Nature – there is no mercy – but not only that: as Francisco González de Canales says – I repeat – 'the great outdoors has been expropriated' as well. In the face of such utter devastation, it would be easy to think of an opposition of a simple Romantic origin: if the sky is filled with jet bombers, if the great outdoors is expropriated, if the fire (not at all Nietzschean, but completely real) spreads everywhere, the cave will be the one that opposes it. This book does not however propose such an easy equation or solution. Undoubtedly, one of the keys to understanding experiments conducted *with life itself*, such as those presented in each chapter, lies in realising that the tremendous destruction brought about by the Second World War is closely linked to the most radical form of technological progress – radical because, like Francisco González de Canales puts it, in no uncertain terms, it is understood in the sense of a huge 'technological party'. The *experimental* houses to which the chapters of this book are devoted are first and foremost experimental *bodies*, but modern bodies all the same: fragmented, braced, technified, dispossessed. Nature, even in places where there is still plenty of evidence of it in all its intensity, whether in the Pacific opposite Isla Negra or the deepest of winter in a Swedish wood – where, in the words of González de Canales, first there was 'desolation' – neither is there, nor can there ever be, any sense of *continuity*, but a break or, in actual fact, the expropriation of the outdoors. None of these houses can be seen as the primitive hut or a shelter for the poor, because none of the inhabitants is still considered to be the lucky soul, or like the Facteur Cheval, 'God's forgotten genius', but rather the opposite, the armed man, the man with body armour: these houses have been designed necessarily to be lived in – although the word is no longer considered to be eloquent – with a solid framework, that is to say, to be scraped and scratched all over. Business as usual. Whatever happens, among the examples chosen with particular skill albeit for different reasons, a certain amount of *bric-à-brac* is detected, not unlike the work of the *bricoleur* that more than one of the key players, fortunately enough, loved a bit too much – too much for the benefit of technology. Some of these houses, and the book makes this patently obvious, still belong to the category of those refuges at the end of the world that are so good at representing the Nautilus or the house of Des Essesintes. Isla Negra, standing full to the brim beside the sea, and exposed to looting, as it was indeed looted, is one of the clearest examples, and one that is also epigonal. The house of O'Gorman in Mexico City and more specifically, as if it were over the top to say so, in San Jerónimo, is another example, albeit more ambiguous, because it has the shape of a cave surrounded by the *imagination* of an overbuilt world. More of these houses, on the other hand, even though they are indeed erected in the depths of the jungle and in winter, as in the case of those of Ralph Erskine, or else in the benign *climate* of California – which is the one determined by the war industry – are built up in the city, right in the heart of the *civitas*, since this is what they have deep inside: *civilised beings*, just like that hound Cerberus. But in any case, this is *civitas umbrae*, no doubt, since he cannot, nor will he conceal the tale with which he describe the Smithson's Fonthill Pavilion, which reveals the great skill on the part of the author of this book: which, almost without thinking, just like art that is born out of art, each chapter had been written in the style of what is being discussed therein. These houses which are so different, that variety of experiments, all come together on the bank of 'civic planning', as Francisco González de Canales has pointed out previously: but this wild side – and this is shown up brilliantly in the book – has been in the centre for ages. What hands were responsible for building the dog's house with four planks of wood? Those of Doctor Livingstone, I presume? No, I suppose not, I fear. The architect's little house, alas, always tilts towards the main building.

The dog's kennel in Villa Vaucresson by Le Corbusier, 1922.

Acknowledgements

Along the line that links together the different cases studies in this book, I have received support from many people; financial, material and intellectual encouragement, without which nothing would have been possible. First of all, I would like to thank the institutions that have supported me financially and institutionally: the Junta de Andalucía, for having me as a scholar during four years and giving me grants and funds, and the La Caixa Foundation, for its grant to study in the United States.

I would also like to thank the institutions, universities and centres that have hosted me. In Spain: my special thanks to the librarians of the Faculty of Architecture of the University of Seville; to the Department of History, Theory and Architectural Composition, for its help on my trips abroad, specially to Victor Pérez Escolano and Javier Rodríguez Barberán, its current director; to the Fidas Foundation in Seville, to its archivist Javier Lobato; to the UPC-ETSAB in Barcelona and the COAC of Catalonia, for allowing me to research the archives of Germán Rodríguez Arias. In the United States: to Harvard University, especially to J. Rafael Moneo, Hashim Sarkis and K. Michael Hays. Also to its librarian and archivist, Inés Zalduendo; to the David Rockefeller Centre for Latin American Studies, to Professor Thomas Cummins; to the Library of the Congress, Washington, to Audrey Fischer; to the Eames Foundation, to Eames Demetrios; to the UCLA, to Sylvia Lavin. In Chile: to the University of Valparaíso, specially to Mirta Halpert, for her dedication, and to Juan Luis Moragas and Gustavo Saavedra, its directors; to the Central University of Santiago, to its director Eliana Israel and to Hernán Montecinos and María Elena Valencia; to the Catholic University of Chile, to Fernando Pérez Oyarzun and Horacio Torrent, to its librarian, Paloma Parrini; to the University of Chile, to Fernán Meza and Patricio Basáez; to the University Diego Portales, for borrowing me the plans of Neruda's houses; to the Pablo Neruda Foundation, to its director Francisco Torres, to Darío Oses, archivist and also to Carolina, Adriana, Cristina and Carmen, for helping me so many days and making my work easier; also to Raúl Bulnes, Assistant Director of the Foundation, for loaning me the plans of the houses that he erected; to the Delia del Carril Foundation, to the architect Carlos Durán, for the donated material. To Ignacio Quintana, devoted companion along my stay in Chile. In Mexico: to the Instituto de Investigaciones Estéticas of the UNAM, to the library and photographic library staff, and, above all, thanks to the generous help of Enrique. To Anda Alanís, without whom I would have been lost in Mexico; to the library of the Architecture Faculty of the UNAM and to the professors Ernesto Alva and Felipe Leal. To the Metropolitan University of Mexico, to Antonio Toca Fernández and the librarian Jacinto Cedeño, for loaning me the material related to O'Gorman's archive. To the Juan Rulfo Foundation, to Víctor Jiménez; to the Diego Rivera and Frida Kahlo Foundation. To the National Museum of Architecture of Mexico, to its director Xavier Guzmán and to the architect Gabriela Grisi, for letting me look through the archives of Juan O'Gorman; to the Luis Cardoza and Aragón Foundation, to Andrea Huerta, for hosting me. To the Berklee College of Music, to Enrique García and María Elena Valádez, for letting me slip in O'Gorman's house. In Sweden: to the architect Ralph Erskine for his great generosity, for the unforgettable gesture of handing me the keys of his house. Also to the staff of the Erskine studio and the Architecture Museum in Stockholm, for its special help, but especially to Cesar Patín Lapausa, for showing me with so much affection and making me discover the complete work of Ralph Erskine in Sweden and inviting me to his house. In England: to the Architectural Association, for giving me so many opportunities, and also to the Sergison Bates in London, and to Simon Smithson, for letting me use his family archives.

I would also like to outstandingly thank the support from those who were my thesis directors. To José Ramón Moreno, loyal companion on this route, for his advice, motivation and discussions together. Also my special thanks to Hashim Sarkis, for his tireless critical spirit and constant support.

I would also like to acknowledge *DC* magazine, from the Architectural Composition Department of the UPC-ETSAB, Barcelona; to *Arquitectura COAM* magazine from the Colegio de Arquitectos of Madrid; to *Metalocus* from Madrid; *RA* from the University of Navarra; *ARQ* from the Catholic University of Chile; *Summa+* in Buenos Aires and the *Journal of Architectural Education* from the College School Association of the United States, for allowing me to expose fragments or seminal articles of the writings that complete this book. Finally to Albert Ferré, Rosa Lleó and Dorota Biczel from Actar, for the help and affection put in this book and to its designer David Lorente.

Special thanks to the valuable comments that I have received about this book from: Félix de Azúa, José Juan Barba, Eve Blau, Iain Borden, Sibel Bozdogan, Luis E. Carranza, George Dodds, Barbara Elfman, Sarah W. Goldhagen, Adrian Gorelik, Xavier Guzmán, K. Michael Hays, Felipe Hernández, Víctor Jiménez, Juan José Lahuerta, Marina Lathouri, Sylvia Lavin, Rafael Moneo, Luis Moreno Mansilla, José Ramón Moreno Pérez, Ann Pendleton-Jullian, Andrés Perea, Victor Pérez Escolano, Fernando Pérez Oyarzun, Antoine Picon, Smiljan Radic, Juan Luis Rodríguez, Graciela Silvestri, Ricardo Sánchez Lampreave, Hashim Sarkis, Eduardo Subirats, Antonio Toca, Horacio Torrent, Emilio Tuñón and Alejandro Von Wareber.

To my parents for educating me and setting me an example, to my sister who helped me with the first translations and, specially, to Nuria, who has helped, loved, and followed me all of this time. Without your help I could not have made it.

Published by
Actar
Barcelona—New York
www.actar.com
info@actar.com

Coordinated by
Albert Ferré
Rosa Lleó

Edited by
Dorota Biczel
Lucy Bullivant

Graphic design and production
ActarPro

Printing and binding
Grafos S.A.

Cover
Charles and Ray Eames, publicity montage for Herman Miller, 1948.
© Eames Office, LLC

ISBN 978-84-92861-65-1
DL B-31218-2012

Printed and bound
in the European Union

Distribution
ActarD
Barcelona—New York
www.actar-d.com

Roca i Batlle 2
E-08023 Barcelona
T +34 93 417 49 93
F +34 93 418 67 07
salesbarcelona@actar.com

151 Grand Street, 5th floor
New York, NY 10013, USA
T +1 212 966 2207
F +1 212 966 2214
salesnewyork@actar.com

Also available in Spanish
Experimentos con la vida misma
ISBN 978-84-92861-66-8